OLDENTREE BIBLIOGRAPHIES
N LANGUAGE AND LITERATURE

$2.95

PAUL L. WILEY

THE
RITISH NOVEL:
CONRAD TO THE PRESENT

The British Novel: Conrad to the Present

GOLDENTREE BIBLIOGRAPHIES IN LANGUAGE AND LITERATURE

under the series editorship of

O. B. HARDISON, JR.

AFRO-AMERICAN WRITERS • Darwin T. Turner

THE AGE OF DRYDEN • Donald F. Bond

AMERICAN DRAMA FROM ITS BEGINNINGS TO THE PRESENT • E. Hudson Long

AMERICAN LITERATURE: POE THROUGH GARLAND • Harry Hayden Clark

AMERICAN LITERATURE THROUGH BRYANT • Richard Beale Davis

THE AMERICAN NOVEL: SINCLAIR LEWIS TO THE PRESENT • Blake Nevius

THE AMERICAN NOVEL THROUGH HENRY JAMES • C. Hugh Holman

THE BRITISH NOVEL: CONRAD TO THE PRESENT • Paul J. Wiley

THE BRITISH NOVEL: SCOTT THROUGH HARDY • Ian Watt

CHAUCER • Albert C. Baugh

LINGUISTICS AND ENGLISH LINGUISTICS • Harold B. Allen

LITERARY CRITICISM: PLATO THROUGH JOHNSON • Vernon Hall

MILTON • James Holly Hanford

OLD AND MIDDLE ENGLISH LITERATURE • William Matthews

ROMANTIC POETS AND PROSE WRITERS • Richard Harter Fogle

THE SIXTEENTH CENTURY: SKELTON THROUGH HOOKER • John L. Lievsay

TUDOR AND STUART DRAMA • Irving Ribner

VICTORIAN POETS AND PROSE WRITERS • Jerome H. Buckley

The British Novel: Conrad to the Present

compiled by

Paul L. Wiley

The University of Wisconsin

AHM PUBLISHING CORPORATION
Northbrook, Illinois 60062

ISBN: 0-88295-530-6

Library of Congress Card Number: 79-178291

PRINTED IN THE UNITED STATES OF AMERICA

713-1

Preface

THE FOLLOWING BIBLIOGRAPHY is intended for graduate and advanced undergraduate students who desire a convenient guide to scholarship in the field of the British novel from the lifetime of Conrad to the present, the terminal point being marked at about 1950. The listing is necessarily selective, but every effort has been made to provide ample coverage of the work of major novelists and also to make place for writers somewhat less celebrated but nevertheless distinctive enough in their own way to reward study. The selection, it is hoped, represents fairly the general range of accomplishment in the novel form within the limits designated and likewise sufficiently recognizes variety in types of individual contribution.

In order to keep this bibliography to a practical size, it has been necessary to omit a number of references: unpublished dissertations; most bibliographies of bibliography; short notes and explications (except when they contain important data); and biographical studies of a commemorative kind. Since all of the novelists included receive at least passing mention in most histories or surveys listed in the general section of the bibliography, it has not seemed essential to repeat mention of such works in the entries for single figures unless treatment proved substantial or of importance in detail. On the principle that the user of the bibliography will be a student rather than a research specialist, the choice of scholarly or critical books and articles under separate authors has been governed by an aim at balanced rather than exhaustive coverage, with a reasonable selection from earlier as well as more recent scholarship. Resulting omissions may be recovered easily through the help of the more extended author bibliographies noted where possible for individual writers. The arrangement in the text section (roughly from the writer's creative work to nonfictional materials) is that of probable importance to the student.

In general, the compiler has attempted to steer a middle course between the brief lists of references included in the average textbook and the long professional bibliography in which significant items are often lost in the sheer number of references given. This bibliography should materially assist the student in his effort to survey a topic, write reports and term papers, prepare for examinations, and do independent reading.

Attention is called to four features intended to enhance its utility:

(1) Extra margin on each page permits listing of library call numbers of often-used items.
(2) Extra space at the botton of every page permits inclusion of additional entries; blank pages for notes follow the final page of entries.
(3) An index by author follows the bibliography proper.
(4) The index and cross reference numbers direct the reader to the page and position-on-the-page of the desired entry. Thus in an entry such as

    HUXLEY, Aldous. "D.H. Lawrence." See 22.5.

    the number 22.5 indicates that the entry referred to is on page 22 and is the fifth item on that page. Both page numbers and individual entry numbers are conspicuous in size and position so that the process of finding entries is fast as well as simple.

An asterisk following an entry indicates a work of special importance, and a dagger (†) indicates that a paperback edition of the book was listed as in print when this bibliography went to press. A parenthetical statement in brackets to clarify a title may also conclude an entry.

Symbols for journals, series, and societies cited herein generally follow the standard forms given at the beginning of recent *PMLA* Bibliographies.

The symbols and their meanings are as follows:

AR	Antioch Review
ArQ	Arizona Quarterly
ASch	American Scholar
AusQ	Australian Quarterly
BA	Books Abroad
BB	Bulletin of Bibliography
BJA	British Journal of Aesthetics (London)
BNYPL	Bulletin of the New York Public Library
BSUF	Ball State University Forum
BuR	Bucknell Review
CE	College English
ChiR	Chicago Review
CJ	Classical Journal
CL	Comparative Literature
Com	Commentary
CR	The Critical Review
Crit	Critique: Studies in Modern Fiction
CritQ	Critical Quarterly
CS	Cahiers du Sud
Cweal	Commonweal

DR	Dalhousie Review
DVLG	Deutsche Vierteljahrsschrift für Literaturwissenschaft und Geistesgeschichte
EA	Etudes anglaises
EDH	Essays by Divers Hands
EFT	English Fiction in Transition (1880-1920) (Purdue Univ.)
EIC	Essays in Criticism (Oxford)
EJ	English Journal
ELH	Journal of English Literary History
ELN	English Language Notes
ELT	English Literature in Transition (1880-1920) (Purdue Univ.) (Formerly English Fiction in Transition; see EFT above.)
EM	English Miscellany
ES	English Studies
E&S	Essays and Studies by Members of the English Association
ESA	English Studies in Africa (Johannesburg)
ESl	Etudes slaves et est-européennes
GaR	Georgia Review
GRM	Germanisch-romanische Monatsschrift, Neue Folge
HudR	Hudson Review
IJES	Indian Journal of English Studies (Calcutta)
JAAC	Journal of Aesthetics and Art Criticism
JEGP	Journal of English and Germanic Philology
JGE	Journal of General Education
JHI	Journal of the History of Ideas
JJR	James Joyce Review
KM	Kansas Magazine
KR	Kenyon Review
LC	Library Chronicle (Univ. of Pa.)
LetN	Lettres nouvelles
LonM	London Magazine
Meanjin	Meanjin Quarterly (U of Melbourne)
MdF	Mercure de France
MFS	Modern Fiction Studies
MinnR	Minnesota Review
MLN	Modern Language Notes
MLQ	Modern Language Quarterly
MLR	Modern Language Review
ModA	Modern Age (Chicago)
MP	Modern Philology
MQ	Midwest Quarterly (Pittsburg, Kans.)
MR	Massachusetts Review (Univ. of Mass.)
NCF	Nineteenth-Century Fiction
NL	Nouvelles littéraires
NM	Neuphilologische Mitteilungen
N&Q	Notes and Queries
NRF	Nouvelle revue française
NS	Die neuren Sprachen
NY	New Yorker
NYHTB	New York Herald Tribune Books
NYTBR	New York Times Book Review

OL	Orbis litterarum
ParR	Paris Review
PBA	Proceedings of the British Academy
PBSA	Papers of the Bibliographical Society of America
PELL	Papers on English Language and Literature (Southern Illinois Univ.)
Per	Perspective (Washington Univ.)
Person	The Personalist
PMASAL	Papers of the Michigan Academy of Science, Arts, and Letters
PMLA	Publications of the Modern Language Association of America
PolR	Polish Review (New York)
PQ	Philological Quarterly (Iowa City)
PR	Partisan Review
PrS	Prairie Schooner
PULC	Princeton University Library Chronicle
QQ	Queen's Quarterly
QR	Quarterly Review
RDM	Revue des deux Mondes
RdP	Revue de Paris
REL	Review of English Literature (Leeds)
Ren	Renascence
RES	Review of English Studies
RLC	Revue de littérature comparée
RLV	Revue des langues vivantes (Brussels)
RMS	Renaissance and Modern Studies (Univ. of Nottingham)
RR	Romanic Review
SAQ	South Atlantic Quarterly
Shen	Shenandoah
SN	Studia neophilologica
SovR	Soviet Review
SP	Studies in Philology
SR	Sewanee Review
SSF	Studies in Short Fiction
SWR	Southwest Review
TamR	Tamarack Review (Toronto)
TArts	Theatre Arts
TC	Twentieth Century
TCL	Twentieth Century Literature
TLS	(London) Times Literary Supplement
TQ	Texas Quarterly (Univ. of Texas)
TSLL	Texas Studies in Literature and Language
UKCR	University of Kansas City Review
UMSE	University of Mississippi Studies in English
UTQ	University of Toronto Quarterly
VQR	Virginia Quarterly Review
WHR	Western Humanities Review
WSCL	Wisconsin Studies in Contemporary Literature (now Contemporary Literature)

WZUR	Wissenschaftliche Zeitschrift der Universität Rostock
XUS	Xavier University Studies
YR	Yale Review
ZAA	Zeitschrift für Anglistik und Amerikanistik (East Berlin)

NOTE: The publisher and compiler invite suggestions for additions to future editions of this bibliography.

Contents

1

Bibliographies

1 *Annual Bibliography of English Language and Literature.* Cambridge: Modern Humanities Research Association, annually since 1920. [Annual volumes include section on twentieth century.] *

2 BATESON, F. W., and George WATSON, eds. *The Cambridge Bibliography of English Literature.* 5 vols. Cambridge: Cambridge U P, 1940, 1957. [Vol. VI, on the modern period, by I. R. Willison, R. J. Roberts, and Charles Corney, in progress.] *

3 BATHO, E. C., and Bonamy DOBREE. *The Victorians and After (1830-1914).* Vol. IV of *Introduction to English Literature.* London: Cresset, 1938; 2d rev. ed., 1950; 3d rev. ed. 1962. [Bibliography includes novelists before 1914.]

4 BELL, Inglis F., and Donald BAIRD. *The English Novel 1578-1956: A Checklist of Twentieth-Century Criticisms.* Denver: Swallow, 1958.

5 BLEILER, Everett F. *The Checklist of Fantastic Literature. A Bibliography of Fantasy, Weird and Science Fiction Books Published in the English Language.* Chicago: Shasta, 1948. [Also Bradford M. Day, *The Supplemental Checklist of Fantastic Literature.* Denver; New York: Science-Fiction and Fantasy Pub., 1963. Mimeographed.]

6 BUFKIN, E. C. *The Twentieth Century Novel in English: A Checklist.* Athens, Ga.: U of Georgia P, 1967.

7 CLARKE, L. F., ed. *The Tale of the Future: From the Beginning to the Present Day, a Checklist.* London: The Library Association, 1961.

8 DAICHES, David. *The Present Age in British Literature.* Bloomington: Indiana U P, 1958. [Includes substantial bibliography of the novel.] *†

9 *English Literature in Transition 1880-1920.* Lafayette, Ind.: English Department, Purdue U, 1957- . [Continuing bibliographies for writers 1880-1920.] *

10 JONES, Claude E. "Modern Books Dealing with the Novel in English: A Check List." *BB* 22(1957):85-7.

11 KERR, Elizabeth. *Bibliography of the Sequence Novel.* Minneapolis: U of Minnesota P, 1950. [British novel, pp. 11-38.]

12 LEARY, Lewis, ed. *Contemporary Literary Scholarship: A Critical Review.* New York: Appleton-Century-Crofts, 1958. [See especially B. A. Booth, "The Novel," pp. 259-88.] *

13 LECLAIRE, L. *A General Analytic Bibliography of the Regional Novelists of the British Isles, 1800-1950.* Paris: Les Belles Lettres, 1954.

14 LEWIS, Arthur O., Jr. "The Anti-Utopian Novel: Preliminary Notes and Checklist." *Extrapolation* 2(1961):27-32.

1 *Modern Fiction Studies.* "Modern Fiction Newsletter." Maurice Beebe. Lafayette, Ind.: Modern Fiction Club of Purdue U, 1955- , especially Winter and Summer issues. [Annotates new studies of fiction.] *

2 *Modern Language Association: Annual Bibliography.* 1919- . [In each May number of *PMLA*. Bibliography international since 1956. Also published in annual volumes as *MLA International Bibliography of Books and Articles on the Modern Languages and Literature*, comp. by Paul A. Brown and Harrison T. Meserole. New York: New York U P; London: U of London P, 1956- .] *

3 PABST, Walter. "Literatur zur Theorie des Romans." *DVLG* 34(1960): 264-89. [Survey article.]

4 ROUSE, H. Blair, et al. "A Selective and Critical Bibliography of Studies in Prose Fiction . . . ." *JEGP* 48(1949):259-84; 49(1950):358-87; 50(1951): 376-407; 51(1952):364-92.

5 SCHOLL, Ralph. "Science Fiction: A Selected Check-List." *BB* 22(1958): 114-5.

6 SOUVAGE, Jacques. "A Systematic Bibliography for the Study of the Novel." Part 2 of *An Introduction to the Study of the Novel.* New York: Humanities, 1965, pp. 103-242.*†

7 STALLMAN, R. W. "A Selected Bibliography of Criticism of Modern Fiction." See 15.16, Aldridge, pp. 553-610.*

8 *The Year's Work in English Studies.* A publication of the English Association of London, 1919- . [Annual bibliographical review of books and articles.] *

Reference Works

9 BAKER, E. A., and James PACKMAN. *A Guide to the Best Fiction: English and American Including Translations from Foreign Languages.* London: Routledge and Paul, 1967.

10 BERGSON, Karl, and Arthur GANZ. *A Reader's Guide to Literary Terms: A Dictionary.* London: Thames and Hudson, 1961.

11 BLUESTONE, George. *Novels into Film.* Berkeley: U of California P, 1966.†

12 BURGESS, Anthony. *The Novel Now: A Student's Guide to Contemporary Fiction.* London: Faber, 1957.†

13 CONNOLLY, Cyril. *The Modern Movement: One Hundred Key Books from England, France, and America, 1880-1950.* London: Deutsch, 1965.

14 COTTON, Gerald, and Alan GLENCROSS. *Fiction Index.* London: Association of Assistant Librarians, 1953. [A guide to over 10,000 works of fiction arranged under 2,000 subject headings.]

3

1 COTTON, Gerald, and Hilda Mary MC GILL. *Fiction Guides General: British and American.* London: Bingley, 1967. [Bibliography of bibliographies and studies.]

2 ELLMANN, Richard, and Charles FEIDELSON, Jr., eds. *The Modern Tradition: Backgrounds of Modern Literature.* New York: Oxford U P, 1965.*

3 *Encyclopedia of World Literature in the Twentieth Century.* 3 vols. Ed. Wolfgang Bernard Fleischmann. New York: Ungar, 1967.*

4 *Everyman's Dictionary of Literary Biography English and American.* Comp. after John W. Cousin by D. C. Browning. London: Dent; New York: Dutton, 1958.

5 FALLS, Cyril. *War Books: A Critical Guide.* London: Davies, 1930. [Includes section on First World War novels.]

6 FIDELL, Estelle A., and Esther V. Flory, eds. *Fiction Catalog.* 7th ed., 1960. New York: Wilson, 1961. Suppl. 1961. Ed. Estelle A. Fidell, New York: Wilson, 1962. Suppl. 1962. Ed. Estelle Fidell, New York: Wilson, 1963. [A list of 4,097 works of fiction in the English language with annotations.]

7 FREEMAN, William. *Dictionary of Fictional Characters.* Boston: The Writer, 1963.

8 GASCOYNE, David. *A Short Survey of Surrealism.* London: Cobden-Sanderson, 1935.

9 GAUNT, William. *The March of the Moderns.* London: Cape, 1949. [Modern movements in art and literature.]

10 GRAVES, Robert, and Alan HODGE. *The Long Week-End: A Social History of Great Britain 1918-1939.* London: Faber and Faber, 1940.*†

11 GRIGSON, Geoffrey, ed. *The Concise Encyclopedia of Modern World Literature.* New York: Hawthorne, 1963.*

12 HARVEY, Paul, comp. and ed. *The Oxford Companion to English Literature.* 4th ed., rev. Oxford: Clarendon P, 1967.

13 KARL, Frederick R., and Marvin MAGALANER. *A Reader's Guide to Great Twentieth-Century English Novels.* New York: Noonday, 1959.†

14 KUNITZ, Stanley J., ed. *Living Authors.* New York: Wilson, 1931.

15 KUNITZ, Stanley J., and Howard HAYCRAFT, eds. *Twentieth Century Authors.* New York: Wilson, 1942; First Supplement, 1955.*

16 LONGAKER, Mark, and Edwin C. BOLLES. *Contemporary English Literature.* New York: Appleton-Century-Crofts, 1953.

17 MC GARRY, Daniel D., and Sarah Harriman WHITE. *Historical Fiction Guide.* New York: Scarecrow, 1963. [Annotated list of 5,000 historical novels.]

18 MILLETT, Fred B. *Contemporary British Literature: A Critical Survey and 235 Author-Bibliographies.* 3d ed. New York: Harcourt, Brace, 1935; rev. and enl., 1950.*

19 NOWELL-SMITH, Simon, ed. *Edwardian England 1901-1914.* London: Oxford U P, 1964.*

1 TAYLOR, A. J. P. *English History 1914-1945.* Oxford: Clarendon P, 1965.*

2 THOMSON, David. *England in the Twentieth Century (1914-65).* Baltimore: Penguin, 1965. †

3 THRALL, William Flint, and Addison HIBBARD. *A Handbook to Literature.* Rev. by C. Hugh Holman. New York: Odyssey, 1960.* †

Literary Histories

4 ALBERES, R. M. *L'aventure intellectuelle du XXe siècle, 1900-1950.* Paris: La Nouvelle Edition, 1950. [English as well as Continental.]

5 ALLSOP, Kenneth. *The Angry Decade: A Survey of the Cultural Revolt of the Nineteen-Fifties.* London: Owen, 1964.

6 BALAKIAN, Nona. "The Flight from Innocence; England's Newest Literary Generation." *Books Abroad* 33(1959):261-70. [1950s.]

7 BAUGH, Albert C., et al. *A Literary History of England.* New York: Appleton-Century-Crofts, 1948.

8 BELL, Quentin. *Bloomsbury.* London: Weidenfeld and Nicolson, 1968.

9 CAZAMIAN, Madeleine. *Le roman et les idées en Angleterre.* 3 vols. Paris: Les Belles Lettres, 1935.*

10 COLLINS, A. S. *English Literature of the Twentieth Century.* With a postscript on the Nineteen-Fifties by Frank Whitehead. London: University Tutorial, 1951, 1961, 1965.

11 DAICHES, David. *A Critical History of English Literature.* 2 vols. New York: Ronald, 1960. [See especially Vol. II, Chap. XIV, "Epilogue: After the Victorians."] *

12 EVANS, B. I. *Literature and Science.* London: Allen and Unwin, 1954.

13 EVANS, B. I. *A Short History of English Literature.* Rev. ed. Baltimore: Penguin, 1968.†

14 FRASER, G. S. *The Modern Writer and His World.* London: Deutsch, 1955.*†

15 GARNETT, David. *The Golden Echo.* 3 vols. Vol. I: *The Golden Echo*; II: *The Flowers of the Forest*; III: *The Familiar Faces.* London: Chatto and Windus, 1953-1962. [Autobiography comments on literary figures of first half of the twentieth century.]

16 HENKIN, Leo J. *Darwinism in the English Novel, 1860-1910: The Impact of Evolution on Victorian Fiction.* New York: Corporate, 1940.

17 HOFFMAN, F. J. *Freudianism and the Literary Mind.* 2d ed., rev. London: Calder, 1959.†

5

1 HOLROYD, Michael. *Lytton Strachey: A Critical Biography.* 2 vols. Vol. I: *The Unknown Years (1880-1910)*; Vol. II: *The Years of Achievement (1910-1932).* London: Heinemann, 1967-1968. [Facts on Strachey's literary milieu.]

2 HOOPS, Reinald. *Der Einflusz der Psychoanalyse auf die englische Literatur.* Heidelberg: Winter, 1934.

3 HOUGH, Graham. *The Dream and the Task: Literature and Morals in the Culture of Today.* London: Duckworth, 1963.

4 HOWARTH, Herbert. *The Irish Writers: Literature and Nationalism, 1880-1940.* New York: Hill and Wang, 1958. [The Parnell legend in Irish literature.] *

5 ISAACS, J. *An Assessment of Twentieth-Century Literature.* London: Secker and Warburg, 1951.

6 JOHNSTONE, J. K. *The Bloomsbury Group: A Study of E. M. Forster, Lytton Strachey, Virginia Woolf, and Their Circle.* New York: Noonday P, 1954, 1963.*

7 LEAVIS, Q. D. *Fiction and the Reading Public.* London: Chatto and Windus, 1932. [Fiction and history of taste since the eighteenth century.]

8 LEGOUIS, Emile, and Louis CAZAMIAN. *A History of English Literature.* New York: Macmillan, 1935; rev. ed., 1957.

9 LEHMANN, John. *The Whispering Gallery: Autobiography 1. I Am My Brother: Autobiography 2. The Ample Proposition: Autobiography 3.* London: Longmans, Green, 1955, 1960, 1966. One vol. ed., *In My Own Time.* Boston: Little, Brown, 1969. [Important for 1930s and '40s.]

10 MOODY, William Vaughan, and Robert M. LOVETT. *A History of English Literature.* Rev. by Fred B. Millett. New York: Scribner's, 1964. †

11 MUCHNIC, Helen. *Dostoevsky's English Reputation: 1881-1936.* Northampton, Mass.: Smith College Studies in Modern Languages XX, 1939.*

12 MUIR, Edwin. *Transition: Essays on Contemporary Literature.* New York: Viking, 1926. [1920s.]

13 O'CONNOR, William Van. *The New University Wits and the End of Modernism.* Carbondale, Ill.: Southern Illinois U P, 1963. [English literary movements after World War II.]

14 PHELPS, Gilbert. *The Russian Novel in English Fiction.* London: Hutchinson, 1956.*

15 ROUTH, H. V. *English Literature and Ideas in the Twentieth Century.* London: Methuen, 1946, 1970.

16 SAMPSON, George. *The Concise Cambridge History of English Literature.* New York: Macmillan, 1941; 3d ed. rev. by R. C. Churchill. New York: Cambridge U P, 1970.†

17 SCOTT-JAMES, R. A. *Fifty Years of English Literature; 1900-1950: With a Postscript–1951 to 1955.* London: Longmans, Green, 1956.

1 SPENDER, Stephen. *The Struggle of the Modern.* Berkeley: U of California P, 1963. [1920s.]†

2 SPIEL, Hilde. *Der Park und die Wildnis: Zur Situation der neueren englischen Literatur.* München: Beck, 1953. [Bowen, Compton-Burnett, Huxley, Mansfield, Morgan, Waugh, Woolf.]

3 STARKIE, Enid. *From Gautier to Eliot: The Influence of France on English Literature 1851-1939.* London: Hutchinson, 1960.

4 STEWART, J. I. M. *Eight Modern Writers.* Vol. XII of *Oxford History of English Literature.* Oxford: Clarendon P, 1963. [Sections on Conrad, Joyce, Lawrence.] *

5 SWINNERTON, Frank. *The Georgian Literary Scene 1910-1935.* Rev. ed. New York: Farrar, Straus, 1950; 2d rev. ed. London: Hutchinson, 1969.

6 SYMONS, Julian. *The Thirties: A Dream Revolved.* London: Cresset, 1960.

7 TAYLOR, Estella R. *The Modern Irish Writers.* Lawrence, Kan.: U of Kansas P, 1954.

8 TINDALL, William York. *Forces in Modern British Literature 1885-1956.* New York: Knopf, 1956.* †

9 VINES, S. *A Hundred Years of English Literature 1830-1940.* London: Duckworth, 1950.

10 WARD, A. C. *The Nineteen-Twenties: Literature and Ideas in the Post-War Decade.* London: Methuen, 1930.

11 WARD, A. C. *Twentieth Century English Literature 1900-1960.* London: Methuen, 1964.

12 WEIMANN, Robert. "Die Literatur der 'Angry Young Men': Ein Beitrag zur Deutung englischer Gegenwartsliteratur." *ZAA* 7(1959):117-89. [1950s.]

13 WELLEK, René. *A History of Modern Criticism, 1750-1950.* 4 vols. New Haven: Yale U P, 1955.*

14 WILSON, Edmund. *Classics and Commercials: A Literary Chronicle of the Forties.* New York: Farrar, Straus and Giroux, 1950.†

15 WILSON, Edmund. *The Shores of Light: A Literary Chronicle of the Twenties and Thirties.* New York: Farrar, Straus and Giroux, 1952.

16 *Writers at Work: The Paris Review Interviews. First Series.* Ed. and Introduction by Malcolm Cowley. *Second Series.* Introduction by Van Wyck Brooks. *Third Series.* Introduction by Alfred Kazin. New York: Viking, 1959-1967.†

Histories of the Novel

17 ALBERES, R. M. *Histoire du roman moderne.* Paris: Michel, 1962.

1 ALLEN, Walter. *The English Novel: A Short Critical History.* London: Phoenix House, 1954; Harmondsworth, Middlesex: Pelican, 1958. †

2 BAKER, E. A. *The History of the English Novel.* 10 vols. New York: Barnes and Noble, 1957. [See Vol. IX: *The Day Before Yesterday*, and Vol. X: *Yesterday*.] *

3 CHURCH, Richard. *Growth of the English Novel.* London: Methuen, 1957. [Handbook-type survey.]

4 CROSS, Wilbur L. *The Development of the English Novel.* New York: Macmillan, 1959.

5 GEROULD, Gordon Hall. *The Patterns of English and American Fiction: A History.* New York: Russell and Russell, 1966. [Chaps. 21 and 22 on Twentieth-century novel.]

6 LOVETT, Robert M., and Helen S. HUGHES. *History of the Novel in England.* New York: Houghton Mifflin, 1932, 1971.

7 NEILL, S. Diana. *A Short History of the English Novel.* London: Jarrolds, 1951; rev. ed., 1964.†

8 STEVENSON, Lionel. *The English Novel: A Panorama.* Boston: Houghton Mifflin, 1960. †

9 WAGENKNECHT, Edward. *Cavalcade of the English Novel.* New York: Holt, 1954.

Period Studies of the Novel

10 ALLEN, Walter. *Tradition and Dream: The English and American Novel from the Twenties to Our Time.* London: Phoenix House, 1964. [Under title *The Modern Novel.* New York: Dutton, 1965.] * †

11 BERGONZI, Bernard. *The Situation of the Novel.* London: Macmillan, 1970.

12 BORINSKI, Ludwig. *Meister des modernen englischen Romans.* Heidelberg: Quelle and Meyer, 1963. [English novel 1890-1950.]

13 BRADY, Charles A. "The British Novel Today." *Thought* 34(1959):518-46. [Post-1940s.]

14 BREWSTER, Dorothy, and Angus BURREL. *Modern Fiction.* New York: Columbia U P, 1934.

15 BURGESS, Anthony. *The Novel Today.* London: Longmans, Green, 1963. [British Council pamphlet. Survey 1930s to 1960s.]

16 CUNLIFFE, J. W. *English Literature in the Twentieth Century.* New York: Macmillan, 1933. [Edwardian and Georgian novelists.]

17 DAICHES, David. *The Novel and the Modern World.* Rev. ed. Chicago: U of Chicago P, 1965. [Extensively rev. from the first ed., 1939.] * †

18 DREW, Elizabeth. *The Modern Novel: Some Aspects of Contemporary Fiction.* New York: Harcourt, Brace, 1926.

8

PERIOD STUDIES OF THE NOVEL

1 ELLIS, G. V. *Twilight on Parnassus: A Study of Post-War Fiction and Pre-War Criticism.* London: Joseph, 1939.

2 EVANS, B. I. *English Literature Between the Wars.* London: Methuen, 1948.*

3 FORD, Boris, ed. *The Modern Age.* Vol. VII of *The Pelican Guide to English Literature.* Harmondsworth, Middlesex: Penguin, 1961.*†

4 FRICKER, Robert. *Der moderne englische Roman.* Göttingen: Vandenhoeck and Ruprecht, 1958. [Survey.]

5 FRIEDMAN, Alan. *The Turn of the Novel: Studies in the Transition to Modern Fiction.* New York: Oxford U P, 1966.†

6 FRIERSON, W. C. *The English Novel in Transition 1885-1940.* Norman, Okla.: U of Oklahoma P, 1942.

7 GLICKSBERG, Charles I. "The Literature of the Angry Young Men." *Chicago Quarterly* 8(1960):293-303.

8 GLICKSBERG, Charles I. "Proletarian Fiction in England." *UTQ* 8(1938-1939):41-55. [Reference to 1930s.]

9 HENDERSON, Philip. *The Novel Today: Studies in Contemporary Attitudes.* London: Lane, 1936. [Chiefly 1930s.]

10 JAMES, Henry. "The New Novel, 1914." *Notes on Novelists and Some Other Notes.* London: Dent, 1914, pp. 314-62.

11 JUMP, John D. "The Recent British Novel." *Memoirs and Proceedings of the Manchester Literary and Philosophical Society* 10(1958-1959):23-28. [Post-1940s.]

12 KIELY, Benedict. *Modern Irish Fiction.* Dublin: Golden Eagle, 1950.*

13 LARRETT, William. *The English Novel from Thomas Hardy to Graham Greene.* Frankfurt am Main: Diesterweg, 1967.

14 LINDSAY, Jack. *After the Thirties: The Novel in Britain and Its Future.* London: Lawrence and Wishart, 1957.

15 MC CORMICK, J. *Catastrophe and Imagination: An Interpretation of the Recent American and English Novel.* London: Longmans, Green, 1957.

16 MACKWORTH, Cecily. "Le roman anglais d'aujourd'hui." *Critique* (Paris) 14, No. 128(1957-1958):32-41. [1950s.]

17 MYERS, Walter L. *The Later Realism: A Study of Characterization in the British Novel.* Chicago: U of Chicago P, 1927. [1920s.] *

18 NEWBY, P. H. *The Novel 1945-50.* London: Longmans, Green, 1951. [British Council pamphlet.]

19 O'CONNOR, Frank. *The Mirror in the Roadway: A Study of the Modern Novel.* London: Hamilton, 1957.

20 O'CONNOR, William Van. "Two Types of 'Heroes' in Post-War British Fiction." *PMLA* 77(1962):168-74. [Post-World War II.]

21 RABINOVITZ, Rubin. *The Reaction Against Experiment in the English Novel, 1950-1960.* New York: Columbia U P, 1967.

1 REED, Henry. *The Novel Since 1939.* London: Longmans, Green, 1946. [British Council pamphlet.]

2 SPENDER, Stephen. *The Creative Element: A Study of Vision, Despair and Orthodoxy Among Some Modern Writers.* London: Hamilton, 1953.*

3 SPENDER, Stephen. *The Destructive Element: A Study of Modern Writers and Beliefs.* London: Cape, 1935. †

4 WEST, Paul. *The Modern Novel.* London: Hutchinson, 1963; 2d ed., 1965. [Chap. on English novelists, pp. 59-153.] *†

5 WILLIAMS, Raymond. *The English Novel from Dickens to Lawrence.* London: Chatto and Windus, 1970.

Studies of Theory

6 ALLOTT, Miriam. *Novelists on the Novel.* London: Routledge and Paul, 1959. [One of the best of this type.] *†

7 AUERBACH, Erich. *Mimesis: The Representation of Reality in Western Literature.* Princeton: Princeton U P, 1953.* †

8 BOOTH, Wayne C. *The Rhetoric of Fiction.* Chicago: U of Chicago P, 1961.*†

9 CHARQUES, R. D. *Contemporary Literature and Social Revolution.* London: Secker, 1933; New York: Haskell House, 1966. [1930s.]

10 COMFORT, Alex. *The Novel and Our Time.* London: Phoenix House, 1948.

11 FORSTER, E. M. *Aspects of the Novel.* London: Arnold, 1927.*†

12 FOX, R. *The Novel and the People.* New York: International Publishers, 1945. [Marxist perspective.]

13 FRYE, Northrop. *Anatomy of Criticism: Four Essays.* New York: Atheneum, 1968. [See especially pp. 263-8 and 303-14.] *†

14 FRYE, Northrop. "The Four Forms of Prose Fiction." *HudR* 2(1950): 582-95.

15 GARDINER, Harold C. *Norms for the Novel.* New York: Hanover House, 1953; rev. ed., 1960.

16 JAMES, Henry. *The Art of the Novel: Critical Prefaces.* Ed. R. P. Blackmur. New York: Scribner's, 1934. [James's prefaces, basic work in contemporary theory.] *†

17 KAYSER, Wolfgang. *Das sprachliche Kunstwerk: Eine Einführung in die Literaturwissenschaft.* Bern: Franke, 1948. [For the novel, see especially pp. 175-84, 262-70, 271-311, 351-68. Theory of European literature.]

18 KERMODE, Frank. *The Sense of an Ending: Studies in the Theory of Fiction.* New York: Oxford U P, 1967. †

10 STUDIES OF THEORY

1 LANGER, Suzanne. *Feeling and Form: A Theory of Art Developed from "Philosophy in a New Key."* New York: Scribner's, 1953. [See especially Chaps. 15, "Virtual Memory," pp. 258-79; and 16, "The Greater Literary Forms," pp. 280-305.] †

2 LEAVIS, F. R. *The Great Tradition.* London: Chatto and Windus, 1948. †

3 LESSER, Simon O. *Fiction and the Unconscious.* Boston: Beacon, 1957.

4 LIDDELL, Robert. *A Treatise on the Novel.* London: Cape, 1947.

5 LUBBOCK, Percy. *The Craft of Fiction.* London: Cape, 1921.* †

6 MILLER, James Edwin, Jr., ed. *Myth and Method: Modern Theories of Fiction.* Lincoln, Neb.: U of Nebraska P, 1960.

7 MONROE, N. Elizabeth. *The Novel and Society: A Critical Study of the Modern Novel.* Port Washington, N.Y.: Kennikat, 1965.

8 MUIR, Edwin. *The Structure of the Novel.* London: Hogarth, 1954.*

9 O'CONNOR, William Van, ed. *Forms of Modern Fiction.* Minneapolis: U of Minnesota P, 1948.* †

10 RALEIGH, John Henry. *Time, Place, and Idea: Essays on the Novel.* Carbondale, Ill.: Southern Illinois U P, 1968.

11 SCHOLES, Robert, ed. *Approaches to the Novel: Material for a Poetics.* San Francisco: Chandler, 1961. †

12 SHRODER, Maurice Z. "The Novel as a Genre." *MR* 4(1963):291-308.

13 SOUVAGE, Jacques. *An Introduction to the Study of the Novel. (With Special Reference to the English Novel.)* New York: Humanities, 1965.* †

14 STANZEL, Franz K. *Typische Formen des Romans.* Göttingen: Vandenhoeck and Ruprecht, 1964. [Typological description.] *

15 STEVIK, Philip, ed. *The Theory of the Novel.* New York: Free P, 1967. †

16 TILLYARD, E. M. W. "The Novel as Literary Kind." *E&S* 9(1956):73-86.

17 VAN GHENT, Dorothy. *The English Novel: Form and Function.* New York: Rinehart, 1961. †

18 VICKERY, John B., ed. *Myth and Literature: Contemporary Theory and Practice.* Lincoln, Neb.: U of Nebraska P, 1966. [Essays on literature and myth.] * †

19 WELLEK, René, and Austin WARREN. *Theory of Literature.* New York: Harcourt, Brace, 1949. [See especially Chap. 16, "The Nature and Modes of Narrative Fiction," pp. 219-34.] * †

20 WILLIAMS, Raymond. "Realism and the Contemporary Novel." *PR* 26(1959):200-13. [Repr. in *The Long Revolution.* London: Chatto and Windus, 1961, Chap. VII.] *

Studies of Form and Narrative

1 BEACH, Joseph Warren. *The Twentieth-Century Novel: Studies in Technique.* New York: Appleton-Century-Crofts, 1932.*

2 BENTLEY, Phyllis. *Some Observations on the Art of Narrative.* London: Home and Van Thal, 1946.*

3 BOWLING, L. E. "What Is Stream of Consciousness Technique?" *PMLA* 65(1950):337-45.

4 BROWN, E. K. *Rhythm in the Novel.* Toronto: U of Toronto P, 1950.†

5 CAZAMIAN, Louis. "Le temps dans le roman anglais contemporain." *EA* 3(1939):338-42.

6 CHURCH, Margaret. *Time and Reality: Studies in Contemporary Fiction.* Chapel Hill: U of North Carolina P, 1963. [Influence of time in the novel.]

7 CLASSE, A. *The Rhythm of English Prose.* Oxford: Blackwell, 1939.

8 CONNOLLY, Cyril. *Enemies of Promise.* Harmondsworth, Middlesex: Penguin, 1961. [See pp. 15-151.] *

9 DOBREE, Bonamy. *Modern Prose Style.* 2d ed. Oxford: Clarendon P, 1964. [See especially Parts IV and V, pp. 211-304.] *

10 DYSON, A. E. *The Crazy Fabric: Essays in Irony.* London: Macmillan, 1965.*

11 EDGAR, Pelham. *The Art of the Novel: From 1700 to the Present Time.* New York: Russell and Russell, 1965.

12 ELLIOTT, Robert C. *The Power of Satire: Magic, Ritual, Art.* Princeton: Princeton U P, 1960.†

13 FORSTER, E. M. *The Development of English Prose Between 1918 and 1939.* Glasgow: Jackson, 1945.

14 FRANK, Joseph. "Spatial Form in the Modern Novel." See 15.16, pp. 43-66.*

15 FRIEDMAN, Melvin. *Stream of Consciousness: A Study in Literary Method.* New Haven: Yale U P, 1955.

16 FRIEDMAN, Norman. "Point of View in Fiction: The Development of a Critical Concept." *PMLA* 70(1955):1160-84.*

17 GORDON, Caroline. *How to Read a Novel.* New York: Viking, 1957.†

18 GRABO, C. H. *The Technique of the Novel.* New York: Scribner's, 1928.

19 HARDY, Barbara. *The Appropriate Form: An Essay on the Novel.* Oxford: Athlone P, 1964.*

12 STUDIES OF FORM AND NARRATIVE

1 HUMPHREY, Robert. *Steam of Consciousness Technique: A Study of James Joyce, Virginia Woolf, Dorothy Richardson, William Faulkner and Others.* Berkeley: U of California P, 1954. †

2 KOHLER, Dayton. "Time in the Modern Novel." *CE* 10(1948-1949):15-24.

3 KUMAR, Shiv K. *Bergson and the Stream of Consciousness Novel.* New York: New York U P, 1963. †

4 LAMMERT, Eberhard. *Bauformen des Erzählens.* Stuttgart: Metzlersche, 1955. [Form of narrative.] *

5 LESSER, Simon O. "The Functions of Form in Narrative Art." *Psychiatry* 18(1955):51-63.

6 LEVIN, Harry. *Symbolism and Fiction.* Charlottesville, Va.: U of Virginia P, 1956.

7 LODGE, David. *Language of Fiction: Essays in Criticism and Verbal Analysis of the English Novel.* New York: Columbia U P, 1966. [Stylistic method.] * †

8 MARTIN, Harold C., ed. *Style in Prose Fiction.* (English Institute Essays, 1958.) New York: Columbia U P, 1959. [Essays on stylistic criticism.]

9 MAYOUX, Jean-Jacques. *Vivants piliers: Le roman anglo-saxon et les symboles.* Paris: Julliard, 1960.

10 MENDILOW, A. A. *Time and the Novel.* New York: Humanities, 1965.*

11 MEYER, K. R. *Zur erlebten Rede im englischen Roman des zwanzigsten Jahrhunderts.* Bern: Francke, 1957.

12 MEYERHOFF, H. *Time in Literature.* Berkeley: U of California P, 1955.*†

13 PASCAL, Roy. "Form and Novel." *MLR* 57(1962):1-11.

14 PAUL, David. "Time and the Novelist." *PR* 21(1954):636-49.

15 RABAN, Jonathan. *The Technique of Modern Fiction: Essays in Practical Criticism.* London: Arnold, 1968. †

16 READ, Herbert. *English Prose Style.* Boston: Beacon, 1955.* †

17 ROMBERG, Bertil. *Studies in Narrative Technique of the First-Person Novel.* Stockholm: Almquist and Wiksell, 1962.*

18 SCHOLES, Robert, and Robert KELLOGG, eds. *The Nature of Narrative.* New York: Oxford U P, 1966.*†

19 SIMON, Irène. *Formes du roman anglais de Dickens à Joyce.* Liège: Faculté de Philosophie et Lettres, 1949.

20 TILLOTSON, Kathleen. *The Tale and the Teller.* London: Hart-Davis, 1959. [On narrator in the novel.]

21 TILLYARD, E. M. W. *The Epic Strain in the English Novel.* London: Chatto and Windus, 1958.*

22 TINDALL, William York. *The Literary Symbol.* New York: Columbia U P, 1955.*

1 WAIN, John. "The Conflict of Forms in Contemporary English Literature." *Essays in Literature and Ideas.* London: Macmillan, 1963, pp. 1-55.

Studies of Genre and Theme

2 ALTER, Robert. *Rogue's Progress: Studies in the Picaresque Novel.* Cambridge, Mass.: Harvard U P, 1964.

3 BEEBE, Maurice. *Ivory Towers and Sacred Founts: The Artist as Hero in Fiction from Goethe to Joyce.* New York: New York U P, 1964.

4 BENTLEY, Phyllis. *The English Regional Novel.* London: Allen and Unwin, 1941. †

5 BLOTNER, Joseph I. *The Political Novel.* Garden City, N.Y.: Doubleday, 1955.

6 BRETNOR, Reginald, ed. *Modern Science Fiction: Its Meaning and Its Forms.* New York: Coward-McCann, 1953.

7 BURGUM, E. B. *The Novel and the World's Dilemma.* New York: Oxford U P, 1947.

8 BUTTERFIELD, Herbert. *The Historical Novel: An Essay.* Cambridge: Cambridge U P, 1924.*

9 CORNWELL, Ethel F. *The Still Point: Themes and Variations in the Writings of T. S. Eliot, Coleridge, Yeats, Henry James, Virginia Woolf and D. H. Lawrence.* New Brunswick: Rutgers U P, 1962.

10 COVENEY, Peter. "Joyce: Virginia Woolf: D. H. Lawrence." *Poor Monkey: The Child in Literature.* London: Rockliff, 1957, pp. 250-81. †

11 COX, C. B. *The Free Spirit: A Study of Liberal Humanism in the Novels of George Eliot, E. M. Forster, Virginia Woolf, Angus Wilson.* London: Oxford U P, 1963.

12 CRAIG, David. "The British Working-Class Novel Today." *ZAA* 11(1963): 29-41. [Allen, Gibbon, Heinemann, Sillitoe, Tressell, Williams.]

13 EDEL, Leon. *The Modern Psychological Novel: 1900-1950.* New York: Lippincott, 1955.

14 FREEDMAN, Ralph. *The Lyrical Novel: Studies in Herman Hesse, André Gide, and Virginia Woolf.* Princeton: Princeton U P, 1963. †

15 GERBER, Richard. *Utopian Fantasy: A Study of English Utopian Fiction Since the End of the Nineteenth Century.* London: Routledge and Paul, 1955.*

16 GILLIE, Christopher. *Character in English Literature.* London: Chatto and Windus, 1965. [See especially Chap. 10 on Joyce and Lawrence, pp. 177-202.]

17 GLICKSBERG, Charles I. *The Self in Modern Literature.* University Park, Pa.: Pennsylvania State U P, 1963.

14 STUDIES OF GENRE AND THEME

1 GOLDBERG, Gerald Jay. "The Search for the Artist in Some Recent British Fiction." *SAQ* 62(1963):387-401. [Beckett, Durrell, Golding, Murdoch.]

2 GREEN, Peter. "Aspects of the Historical Novel." *EDH* 31(1962):35-60.

3 GREGOR, Ian, and Brian NICHOLAS. *The Moral and the Story.* London: Faber and Faber, 1962. [Ethical questions in the novel.]

4 HARVEY, W. J. *Character and the Novel.* Ithaca, N.Y.: Cornell U P, 1965.*†

5 HIGHET, Gilbert. *The Anatomy of Satire.* Princeton: Princeton U P, 1962. [*Passim* for contemporary satire in the novel.] *

6 HOFFMAN, F. J. *The Mortal No: Death and the Modern Imagination.* Princeton: Princeton U P, 1964. [Conrad, Forster, Joyce, Lawrence, Woolf.]

7 HOWE, Irving. *Politics and the Novel.* New York: Horizon, 1957.†

8 HOWE, Susanne. *Novels of Empire.* New York: Columbia U P, 1949.

9 HUGHES, D. J. "Character in Contemporary Fiction." *MR* 3(1962):788-95.

10 KILLINGER, John. *The Failure of Theology in Modern Literature.* New York: Abingdon, 1963.

11 KRIEGER, Murray. *The Tragic Vision: Variations on a Theme in Literary Interpretation.* Chicago: Chicago U P, 1966. [Conrad, Lawrence.] * †

12 LECLAIRE, L. *Le Roman Régionaliste dans les Iles Britanniques (1800-1950).* Paris: Les Belles Lettres, 1954.

13 LEWIS, R. W. B. *The Picaresque Saint: Representative Figures in Contemporary Fiction.* New York: Lippincott, 1959.*

14 LUKACS, George. *The Historical Novel.* London: Merlin, 1962. [Significant Marxist treatment of European historical novel.] *†

15 MAC NEICE, Louis. *Varieties of Parable.* New York: Cambridge U P, 1963.*

16 MAYOUX, Jean-Jacques. *L'inconscient et la vie intérieure dans la roman anglais: 1905-1940.* Nancy: Centre Européen Universitaire, 1952.

17 MELCHIORI, Giorgio. *The Tightrope Walkers: Studies of Mannerism in Modern English Literature.* London: Routledge and Paul, 1956.*

18 MOSKOWITZ, Sam. *Explorers of the Infinite: Shapers of Science Fiction.* Cleveland: World Publishing, 1963.†

19 MUELLER, William R. *The Prophetic Voice in Modern Fiction.* New York: Association, 1959. [Six novels in relation to the Bible.]

20 MULLER, H. J. *Modern Fiction: A Study of Values.* New York: McGraw-Hill, 1964.*

21 MURCH, A. E. *The Development of the Detective Novel.* London: Owen, 1958.

1 NICOLSON, Marjorie Hope. *Voyages to the Moon.* New York: Macmillan, 1948.†

2 O'DONNELL, D. *Maria Cross: Imaginative Patterns in a Group of Modern Catholic Writers.* New York: Oxford U P, 1952; London: Burns and Oates, 1963. [Under name Conor Cruise O'Brien.] *

3 O'FAOLAIN, Sean. *The Vanishing Hero: Studies in the Novels of the Twenties.* Boston: Little, Brown, 1957. [Bowen, Greene, Huxley, Joyce, Waugh, Woolf.] *

4 PASCAL, Roy. *Design and Truth in Autobiography.* London: Routledge and Paul, 1960. [See especially Chap. 11, "The Autobiographical Novel."] *

5 PENDRY, E. D. *The New Feminism of English Fiction: A Study of Contemporary Women-Novelists.* Tokyo: Kenkyusha, 1956.

6 PENZOLDT, Peter. *The Supernatural in Fiction.* New York: Humanities, 1965.

7 PROCTOR, M. R. *The English University Novel.* Berkeley: U of California P, 1957.

8 SCARBOROUGH, Dorothy. *The Supernatural in Modern English Fiction.* London: Putnam, 1917.

9 SEWARD, Barbara. *The Symbolic Rose.* New York: Columbia U P, 1960, pp. 127-43. [Novelists.]

10 SINGER, Godfrey Frank. *The Epistolary Novel: Its Origin, Development, Decline and Residuary Influence.* Philadelphia: U of Pennsylvania P, 1933.

11 SPEARE, Morris E. *The Political Novel: Its Development in England and in America.* New York: Oxford U P, 1924. [Early definition of genre.]

12 TYMMS, Ralph. *Doubles in Literary Psychology.* Cambridge: Bowes and Bowes, 1949. [Doppelgänger theme.] *

13 WARNER, Rex. *The Cult of Power.* Philadelphia: Lippincott, 1947. [On allegorical method.] *

14 WEST, Katharine. *Chapter of Governesses: A Study of the Governess in English Fiction.* London: Cohen and West, 1949.

15 WOODCOCK, George. *The Writer and Politics.* London: Porcupine, 1948.

Collections of Studies: Twentieth-Century Novel

16 ALDRIDGE, John W., ed. *Critiques and Essays on Modern Fiction.* New York: Ronald, 1952.*

17 DAVIE, Donald, ed. *Russian Literature and Modern English Fiction.* Chicago: U of Chicago P, 1965.†

18 DAVIS, Robert Murray, ed. *The Novel: Modern Essays in Criticism.* Englewood Cliffs, N.J.: Prentice-Hall, 1969. †

16 COLLECTIONS OF STUDIES: TWENTIETH-CENTURY NOVEL

1 GINDIN, James. *Postwar British Fiction.* Berkeley: U of California P, 1962. [Post-World War II.]

2 HALL, James. *The Tragic Comedians.* Bloomington: Indiana U P, 1963. [Cary, Forster, Green, Hartley, Huxley, Powell, Waugh.]

3 HARDY, John Edward. *Man in the Modern Novel.* Seattle: U of Washington P, 1964. [Conrad, Forster, Joyce, Lawrence, Waugh, Woolf.] †

4 HOARE, Dorothy M. *Some Studies in the Modern Novel.* Philadelphia: Dufour, 1953.*

5 KARL, Frederick. *The Contemporary English Novel.* New York: Farrar, Straus and Giroux, 1962.

6 KERMODE, Frank. *Puzzles and Epiphanies, Essays and Reviews 1958-1961.* London: Routledge and Paul, 1962.

7 KETTLE, Arnold. *An Introduction to the English Novel.* 2 vols. London: Hutchinson, 1953. [Vol. 2: *Henry James to the Present.*] *†

8 MOONEY, Harry J., and Thomas F. STALEY, eds. *The Shapeless God: Essays on Modern Fiction.* Pittsburgh: U of Pittsburgh P, 1969.

9 OPPEL, Horst, ed. *Der moderne englische Roman: Interpretationen.* Berlin: Schmidt, 1965. [Interpretations of modern English novels.]

10 "Perspectives on the Novel." *Daedalus: Journal of the American Academy of Arts and Sciences.* 92(Spring 1963), 312-29.

11 PRITCHETT, V. S. *The Living Novel and Later Appreciations.* New York: Random House, 1964.*

12 RAJAN, B., ed. *Focus Four: The Novelist as Thinker.* London: Dobson, 1947. [Huxley, Isherwood, Myers, Waugh.]

13 RIPPIER, Joseph S. *Some Postwar English Novelists.* Frankfurt am Main: Diesterweg, 1965. [Post-World War II.]

14 SAVAGE, D. S. *The Withered Branch: Six Studies in the Modern Novel.* London: Eyre and Spottiswoode, 1950. [Forster, Huxley, Joyce, Woolf.]

15 SCHORER, Mark, ed. *Modern British Fiction: Essays in Criticism.* New York: Oxford U P, 1961. [Conrad, Ford, Forster, Huxley, Joyce, Lawrence, Woolf.] †

16 SHAPIRO, Charles, ed. *Contemporary British Novelists.* Carbondale, Ill.: Southern Illinois U P, 1965. [Novelists since World War II: Amis, Durrell, Golding, Lessing, Murdoch, Powell, Sillitoe, Snow, Spark, Wilson.] †

17 VERSCHOYLE, Derek, ed. *The English Novelists: A Survey of the Novel by Twenty Contemporary Novelists.* London: Chatto and Windus, 1936.

18 WEST, R. B., and R. W. STALLMAN, eds. *The Art of Modern Fiction.* New York: Rinehart, 1949. †

19 ZABEL, M. D. *Craft and Character: Texts, Methods, and Vocation in Modern Fiction.* New York: Viking, 1957.*

British Novelists

Arnold Bennett (1867-1931)

TEXTS

1 *The Minerva Edition of the Works of Arnold Bennett.* 7 vols. London: Library, 1926. [*Anna of the Five Towns, Teresa of Watling Street, A Great Man, Whom God Hath Joined, Buried Alive, The Card, The Regent.*]

2 *The Clayhanger Family.* London: Methuen, 1925. [*Clayhanger, Hilda Lessways*, and *These Twain.*]

3 *The Arnold Bennett Omnibus Book.* London: Cassell, 1931. [*Riceyman Steps*, "Elsie and the Child," *Lord Raingo*, and *Accident.*]

4 *Anna of the Five Towns. Clayhanger. The Grand Babylon Hotel. The Old Wives' Tale. Riceyman Steps.* Ed. Frank Swinnerton. London: Penguin, 1954.

5 *The Old Wives' Tale.* Preface by Bennett. New York: Random House [Modern Library], (196?).

6 *Riceyman Steps and Elsie and the Child.* Introduction by Michael Sadleir. London: Collins, 1956.

7 *Tales of the Five Towns, including "The Grim Smile of the Five Towns."* London: Chatto and Windus, 1964.

8 *The Author's Craft and Other Critical Writings of Arnold Bennett.* Ed. Samuel Hynes. Lincoln, Neb.: U of Nebraska P, 1968.†

9 *Arnold Bennett's Letters to His Nephew.* Ed. Richard Bennett. Preface by Frank Swinnerton. London: Heinemann, 1936.

10 *Arnold Bennett and H. G. Wells: The Record of a Personal and Literary Friendship.* Ed. Harris Wilson. Urbana, Ill.: U of Illinois P, 1959. [Letters.]

11 *Letters of Arnold Bennett.* Ed. James Hepburn. Vol. I: *Letters to J. B. Pinker.* Vol. II: *1889-1915.* Vol. III: *1916-1931.* London: Oxford U P, 1966-1970. [Vol. IV i preparation, being Bennett's letters to his family.]

12 *Journal 1929.* London: Cassell, 1930.*

13 *The Journals of Arnold Bennett.* Ed. Newman Flower. 3 vols. London: Cassell, 1932-1933. [Valuable comments by Bennett on his theories of art.] *

14 *The Journal of Arnold Bennett, 1896-1928.* New York: Viking, 1933. [A reediting of the Flower edition "for American readers."] *

18

BIBLIOGRAPHIES

1 EMERY, Norman. *Arnold Bennett (1867-1931): A Bibilography.* Hanley, Stoke-On-Trent: Central Library, 1967. [Horace Barks Reference Library, Bibliographical Series No. 3, 1967.] *

2 HEPBURN, James G. "Selected Annotated Bibliography of Arnold Bennett." *EFT* 1(1957):8-12. [*EFT* has continuing bibliography on Bennett since 1957. See also 18.5, pp. 222-38.] *

CRITICAL AND BIOGRAPHICAL BOOKS

3 ALLEN, Walter. *Arnold Bennett.* Denver: Swallow, 1949.

4 HALL, James. *Arnold Bennett: Primitivism and Taste.* Seattle: U of Washington P, 1959.

5 HEPBURN, James G. *The Art of Arnold Bennett.* Bloomington: Indiana U P, 1963.*

6 LAFOURCADE, Georges. *Arnold Bennett, A Study.* London: Muller, 1939.*

7 POUND, Reginald. *Arnold Bennett.* New York: Harcourt, Brace, 1953. [Biography.] *

8 SIMONS, J. B. *Arnold Bennett and His Novels.* Oxford: Blackwell, 1936.

9 WEST, Geoffrey (Geoffrey H. Wells). *The Problem of Arnold Bennett.* London: Joiner and Steele, 1932.

10 WOOLF, Virginia. *Mr. Bennett and Mrs. Brown.* London: Hogarth, 1928. [First published 1924. Repr. in 114.15, Vol. I, pp. 319-37.] *

CRITICAL ESSAYS

11 BEACH, Joseph Warren. "Variations: Bennett." See 11.1, pp. 231-45.*

12 DREW, Elizabeth. See 7.18, pp. 199-219.

13 DUTTON, George B. "Arnold Bennett, Showman." *SR* 33(1925):64-72.

14 HEPBURN, James G. "The Notebook for *Riceyman Steps.*" *PMLA* 78(1963):257-61.

15 HYNES, Samuel. "The Whole Contention Between Mr. Bennett and Mrs. Woolf." *Novel* 1(1967):34-44.

16 KENNEDY, James G. "Arnold Bennett: Künstler and Bürger." *EFT* 5(1962):1-20.

17 KENNEDY, James G. "Reassuring Facts in *The Pretty Lady, Lord Raingo,* and Modern Novels." *EFT* 7(1964):131-42.

1 PRIESTLEY, J. B. "Mr. Arnold Bennett." *London Mercury* 9(1924): 394-406.

2 PRITCHETT, V. S. "The Five Towns." See 16.11, pp. 169-175.

3 SHERMAN, Stuart P. "The Realism of Arnold Bennett." *On Contemporary Literature.* New York: Holt, 1917, pp. 102-19.

4 SITWELL, Sir Osbert. "Arnold Bennett." *Nobel Essences.* Boston: Little, Brown, 1950, pp. 317-34.

5 TILLYARD, E. M. W. "Middlemarch and Bursley." See 12.21, pp. 168-86.*

6 WAIN, John. "The Quality of Arnold Bennett." *Preliminary Essays.* London: Macmillan, 1957, pp. 121-56.*

7 WEST, Rebecca. "Uncle Bennett." *The Strange Necessity.* Garden City, N.Y.: Doubleday, Doran, 1928, pp. 215-31.

Elizabeth Bowen (1899-)

TEXTS

8 The Collected Edition. London: Jonathan Cape, 1948- . [Includes principal works by Elizabeth Bowen.]

9 *Collected Impressions.* London: Longmans, Green, 1950. [Contains some statements of theory.]

10 *After-Thought: Pieces About Writing.* London: Longmans, Green, 1962.

11 *Why Do I Write? An Exchange of Views Between Elizabeth Bowen, Graham Greene, and V. S. Pritchett.* London: Marshall, 1948.

12 *Seven Winters: Memories of a Dublin Childhood.* London: Longmans, Green, 1943.

13 "Coming to London, 6." *Coming to London.* Ed. John Lehmann. London: Phoenix House, 1957, pp. 74-81. [Autobiographical section by Elizabeth Bowen.]

BIBLIOGRAPHIES

14 HEATH, William. "Selected Bibliography." See 19.16, pp. 170-6.

CRITICAL AND BIOGRAPHICAL BOOKS

15 BROOKE, Jocelyn. *Elizabeth Bowen.* London: Longmans, Green, 1952. [British Council pamphlet.]

16 HEATH, William. *Elizabeth Bowen: An Introduction to Her Novels.* Madison: U of Wisconsin P, 1961.

CRITICAL ESSAYS

17 DAICHES, David. "The Novels of Elizabeth Bowen." *EJ* 38(1949):305-13.*

18 GREENE, George. "Elizabeth Bowen: Imagination as Therapy." *Per* 14(1965):42-52.

19 GREENE, Graham. "The Dark Backward: A Footnote." *London Mercury* 32(1935):562-5.

1 HALL, James. "The Giant Located: Elizabeth Bowen." *The Lunatic Giant in the Drawing Room: The English and American Novel Since 1930.* Bloomington: Indiana U P, 1968, pp. 17-55.

2 HARDWICK, Elizabeth. "Elizabeth Bowen's Fiction." *PR* 16(1949): 1114-21.

3 HARKNESS, Bruce. "The Fiction of Elizabeth Bowen." *EJ* 44(1955): 499-506.

4 KARL, Frederick R. "The World of Elizabeth Bowen." See 16.5, pp. 107-30.

5 MITCHELL, Edward. "Themes in Elizabeth Bowen's Short Stories." *Crit* 8(1966):41-54.

6 O'FAOLAIN, Sean. "Elizabeth Bowen, or Romance Does Not Pay." See 15.3, pp. 167-90.

7 PENDRY, E. D. "Elizabeth Bowen." See 15.5, pp. 120-52.

8 PRITCHETT, V. S. "The Future of English Fiction." *PR* 15(1948):1063-70.

9 RUPP, Richard Henry. "The Post-War Fiction of Elizabeth Bowen." *XUS* 4(1965):55-67.

10 SACKVILLE-WEST, Edward. "Ladies Whose Bright Pens . . . ." *Inclinations.* London: Secker and Warburg, 1949, pp. 78-103.*

11 SEWARD, Barbara. "Elizabeth Bowen's World of Impoverished Love." *CE* 18(1956):30-7.*

12 SHARP, Sister M. Corona, O.S.U. "The House as Setting and Symbol in Three Novels by Elizabeth Bowen." *XUS* 2(1963):93-103.

13 SNOW, Lotus. "The Uncertain 'I': A Study of Elizabeth Bowen's Fiction." *WHR* 4(1950):299-310.

14 STRONG, L. A. G. *Personal Remarks.* New York: Liveright, 1953, pp. 132-45.

15 VAN DUYN, Mona. "Pattern and Pilgrimage: A Reading of *The Death of the Heart.*" *Crit* 4(1961):52-66.

16 WAGNER, Geoffrey. "Elizabeth Bowen and the Artificial Novel." *EIC* 13(1963):155-63.*

17 WILLIAMS, Raymond. "Realism and the Contemporary Novel." *PR* 26(1959):200-13.

18 WYNDHAM, Francis. *The Craft of Letters in England.* Ed. John Lehmann. London: Cresset, 1956, pp. 46-51.

Joyce Cary (1888-1957)

TEXTS

19 The Carfax Edition. London: Michael Joseph, 1951-1954. [All novels except *Except the Lord, Not Honour More, The Captive and the Free.* Each volume has a preface by Cary with important statements on treatment and method.] *

1 *The Horse's Mouth.* Ed. Andrew Wright. London: Rainbird and Joseph, 1957. [Authoritative text with supplementary material and bibliography.]

2 *First Trilogy: Herself Surprised, To Be a Pilgrim, The Horse's Mouth.* New York: Harper, 1958. [New Cary preface. Changes and corrections by Cary and Andrew Wright in text of *The Horse's Mouth.*]

3 *The Horse's Mouth.* Introduction by Andrew Wright. New York: Harper's Modern Classics, 1959. [Also in Universal Library.]

4 *Herself Surprised.* Supplementary note by Andrew Wright. New York: Harper's Modern Classics, 1961.

5 *The Captive and the Free.* Editor's note by Winifred Davin. Introduction by Lord David Cecil. London: Joseph; New York: Harper, 1959.

6 *Power in Men.* Ed. Hazard Adams. London: Nicholson and Watson, 1939; Seattle: U of Washington P, 1963.

7 *Memoir of the Bobotes.* Introductory note by James B. Meriwether. Austin: U of Texas P, 1960. [Memoirs of First Balkan War, 1912-13.]

BIBLIOGRAPHIES

8 ADAMS, Hazard. "Joyce Cary: Posthumous Volumes and Criticism to Date." *TSLL* 1(1959):289-99.*

9 BEEBE, Maurice, James W. LEE, and Sam HENDERSON. "Criticism of Joyce Cary: A Selected Checklist." *MFS* 9(1963):284-8.

10 MERIWETHER, James B. "The Books of Joyce Cary: A Preliminary Bibliography of English and American Editions." *TSLL* 1(1959):300-10.

11 WRIGHT, Andrew. "Bibliography." See 21.18, pp. 174-81.

12 WRIGHT, Andrew, cataloguer. *Hand List of the Joyce Cary Manuscripts of James M. Osborn Deposited in the Bodleian Library, Oxford.* 1958. [For research in primary manuscript and notebook materials.]

CRITICAL AND BIOGRAPHICAL BOOKS

13 ALLEN, Walter. *Joyce Cary.* London: Longmans, Green, 1953; rev. 1954, 1956, 1963.*†

14 FOSTER, Malcolm. *Joyce Cary: A Biography.* Boston: Houghton Mifflin, 1968.

15 HOFFMANN, Charles G. *Joyce Cary: The Comedy of Freedom.* Pittsburgh: U of Pittsburgh P, 1964.*

16 MAHOOD, M. M. *Joyce Cary's Africa.* London: Methuen, 1964.*

17 WOLKENFELD, Jack. *Joyce Cary: The Developing Style.* New York: New York U P, 1968.

18 WRIGHT, Andrew. *Joyce Cary: A Preface to His Novels.* London: Chatto and Windus, 1959.*

CRITICAL ESSAYS

The first two titles are collections of critical essays in special numbers of journals.

1 *Adam International Review* 18, Nos. 212-3(1950). Joyce Cary Special Issue. [Includes Joyce Cary, "The Way a Novel Gets Written," pp. 3-10; "The Novelist at Work: A Conversation Between Joyce Cary and Lord David Cecil," pp. 15-25; and other critical essays.]

2 *MFS* 9(1963). Joyce Cary Special Number. [Essays by nine contributors.]

3 ADAMS, Hazard. "Blake and Gulley Jimson: English Symbolists." *Crit* 3(1959):3-14.*

4 ADAMS, Hazard. "Joyce Cary's Three Speakers." *MFS* 5(1959):108-20.

5 ADAMS, Robert M. "Freedom in *The Horse's Mouth.*" *CE* 26(1965): 451-60.

6 BETTMAN, Elizabeth R. "Joyce Cary and the Problem of Political Morality." *AR* 17(1957):266-72.

7 BURROWS, John, and Alex HAMILTON. "The Art of Fiction: VII: Joyce Cary." *ParR* 7(Fall-Winter 1954-1955):63-78. Repr. in 6.16, First Series, pp. 51-67. [Interview.]

8 CASE, Edward. "The Free World of Joyce Cary." *ModA* 3(1959):115-24.

9 COHEN, Nathan. "A Conversation with Joyce Cary." *TamR* 3(1957):5-15. [Interview.]

10 GARANT, Jeanne. "Joyce Cary's Portrait of the Artist." *RLV* 24(1958): 476-86.

11 HALL, James. "Directed Restlessness: Joyce Cary." See 16.2, pp. 82-98.

12 HARDY, Barbara. "Form in Joyce Cary's Novels." *EIC* 4(1954):180-90.*

13 JOHNSON, Pamela Hansford. "Three Novelists and the Drawing of Character: C. P. Snow, Joyce Cary and Ivy Compton-Burnett." *E&S* 3(1950): 89-91.

14 KARL, Frederick R. "Joyce Cary: The Moralist as Novelist." See 16.5, pp. 131-47. Also in *TCL* 5(1960):183-96.

15 KERR, Elizabeth M. "Joyce Cary's Second Trilogy." *UTQ* 29(1960):310-25.

16 KETTLE, Arnold. "Joyce Cary: Mister Johnson." See 16.7, II, pp. 177-84.

17 REED, Peter J. "Holding Back: Joyce Cary's *To Be a Pilgrim.*" *WSCL* 10(1969):103-16.

18 RYAN, Marjorie. "An Interpretation of Joyce Cary's *The Horse's Mouth.*" *Crit* 2(1958):29-38.

19 SEYMOUR-SMITH, Martin. "Zero and the Impossible." *Encounter* 9(1957): 45-7.

1 STARKIE, Enid. "Joyce Cary: A Personal Portrait." *VQR* 37(1961):110-34.

2 WATSON, Kenneth. " 'The Captive and the Free': Artist, Child, and Society in the World of Joyce Cary." *English* 16(1966-1967):49-54.

3 WEST, Anthony. "Books: Footloose and Fancy-Free." *NY* 36(April 30, 1960):170-6.

4 WRIGHT, Andrew. "Joyce Cary's Unpublished Work." *LonM* 5(January 1958):35-42.*

Ivy Compton-Burnett (1892-1969)

TEXTS

There is no collected edition, but Miss Compton-Burnett's first novel, *Dolores*, and her last, *The Last and the First* (completed by others from Miss Compton-Burnett's notebooks), were in 1971 added to her eighteen novels already in print.

BIBLIOGRAPHIES

5 BALDANZA, Frank. "Selected Bibliography." See 23.6, pp. 135-8. [Annotated bibliography.]

CRITICAL AND BIOGRAPHICAL BOOKS

6 BALDANZA, Frank. *Ivy Compton-Burnett.* New York: Twayne, 1964.

7 BURKHART, Charles. *I. Compton-Burnett.* London: Gollancz, 1965.*

8 JOHNSON, Pamela Hansford. *I. Compton-Burnett.* London: Longmans, Green, 1951. [British Council pamphlet.]

9 LIDDELL, Robert. *The Novels of Ivy Compton-Burnett.* London: Gollancz, 1955.*

CRITICAL ESSAYS

10 AMIS, Kingsley. "One World and Its Way." *TC* 158(1955):168-75.

11 BOWEN, Elizabeth. "Ivy Compton-Burnett." See 19.9, pp. 82-91.

12 "A Conversation Between I. Compton-Burnett and M. Jourdain." *Orion, A Miscellany.* Vol. I. London: Nicholson àn;Watson, 1945, pp. 20-8.

13 CRANSTON, Maurice. "Ivy Compton-Burnett." Trans. Renée Villoteau. *LetN* 64(1958):425-40.

14 GREENFIELD, Stanley B. "Pastors and Masters: The Spoils of Genius." *Criticism* 2(1960):66-80.

15 "Interview with Miss Compton-Burnett." *REL* 3(1962):96-112.

16 ISER, Wolfgang. "Ivy Compton-Burnett: A Heritage and Its History." See 16.9, Oppel, pp. 376-98.

1 JEFFERSON, D. W. "A Note on Ivy Compton-Burnett." *REL* 1(1960): 68-80.

2 JOHNSON, Pamela Hansford. "Three Novelists and the Drawing of Character: C. P. Snow, Joyce Cary and Ivy Compton-Burnett." *E&S* 3(1950): 82-99.

3 KERMODE, Frank. "The House of Fiction: Interviews with Seven English Novelists." *PR* 30(1963):61-82.

4 KETTLE, Arnold. "I. Compton-Burnett: A Family and a Fortune." See 16.7, II, pp. 184-90.

5 KUNITZ, Stanley J., and Howard HAYCRAFT, eds. See 3.15, First Supplement.

6 MC CABE, Bernard. "Ivy Compton-Burnett, an English Eccentric." *Crit* 3(1960):47-63.

7 MC CARTHY, Mary. "The Inventions of I. Compton-Burnett." *Encounter* 27(1966):19-31.*

8 NEWBY, P. H. See 8.18, pp. 29-31.

9 PENDRY, E. D. "Ivy Compton-Burnett." See 15.5, pp. 90-119.

10 PHELPS, Gilbert. "The Novel Today." See 8.3, Ford, pp. 476-9.

11 PRESTON, John. "The Matter in a Word." *EIC* 10(1960):348-56.

12 SACKVILLE-WEST, Edward. See 20.10, pp. 78-103.

13 SARRAUTE, Nathalie. *The Age of Suspicion.* New York: Braziller, 1963, pp. 112-7.

14 STRACHEY, Richard. "The Works of Ivy Compton-Burnett." *Life and Letters* 12(1935):30-6.

15 WEST, Anthony. "Ivy Compton-Burnett." *Principles and Persuasions.* New York: Harcourt, Brace, 1957, pp. 225-32.

16 WILSON, Angus. "Ivy Compton-Burnett." *LonM* 2(1955):64-70.*

Joseph Conrad (1857-1924)

TEXTS

17 *The Works of Joseph Conrad.* 20 vols. London: Heinemann, 1921-1927. [A limited edition. Conrad made revisions in the text and contributed author's notes.]

18 *The Works of Joseph Conrad.* Uniform Edition. 22 vols. London: Dent, 1923-1928. [A general edition. Complete except the plays: *The Secret Agent –A Drama, Laughing Anne,* and *One Day More.* Conrad took great interest in this edition, which includes his prefatory notes.]

1 *The Works of Joseph Conrad.* New Collected Edition. 21 vols. London: Dent, 1946- . [A reissue of the Dent Uniform with prefatory notes by Conrad but omits *The Inheritors.*]

2 *The Sisters.* Introduction by Ford Madox Ford. New York: Gaige, 1928. [Fragment of an unfinished novel.]

3 *Nostromo.* Introduction by Robert Penn Warren. New York: Modern Library, 1951.

4 *Under Western Eyes.* Introduction by Morton Dauwen Zabel. Garden City, N.Y.: Doubleday, 1963.†

5 *The Portable Conrad.* Ed. with introduction and notes by Morton Dauwen Zabel. New York: Viking, 1947; rev. ed., 1968.†

6 *Heart of Darkness: An Authoritative Text, Backgrounds and Sources, Essays in Criticism.* Ed. Robert Kimbrough. New York: Norton, 1963. [Essays by various hands.] †

7 *Conrad's Prefaces to His Works. With an Introductory Essay by Edward Garnett and a Biographical Note on His Father by David Garnett.* London: Dent, 1937.*

8 *Joseph Conrad on Fiction.* Ed. Walter F. Wright. Lincoln, Neb.: U of Nebraska P, 1964. [Full selection of Conrad's essays on books and authors, his literary reminiscences, and his prefaces, also annotated excerpts from published letters.] †

9 AUBRY, G. J. *Joseph Conrad: Life and Letters.* 2 vols. Garden City, N.Y.: Doubleday, Doran, 1927.

10 CURLE, R., ed. *Conrad to a Friend.* New York: Gaige, 1928. [Letters of Conrad to Richard Curle.]

11 GARNETT, Edward, ed. *Letters from Joseph Conrad, 1895-1924.* Introduction and notes by Garnett. Bloomsbury, London: Nonesuch, 1928.*

12 *Letters of Joseph Conrad to Marguerite Poradowska 1890-1920.* Ed. J. A. Gee and P. J. Sturm. New Haven: Yale U P, 1940.*

13 BLACKBURN, W., ed. *Joseph Conrad: Letters to William Blackwood and David S. Meldrum.* Durham, N.C.: Duke U P, 1958.*

14 NAJDER, Zdzislaw, ed. *Conrad's Polish Background: Letters to and from Polish Friends.* London: Oxford U P, 1964.

BIBLIOGRAPHIES

15 BOJARSKI, E. A., and Henry T. BOJARSKI. *Joseph Conrad: A Bibliography of Masters' Theses and Doctoral Dissertations, 1917-1963.* Lexington, Ky.: U of Kentucky Libraries, 1964. [Occasional Contribution, No. 157.]

16 EHRSAM, Theodore. *A Bibliography of Joseph Conrad.* Metuchen, N.J.: Scarecrow, 1969. [Includes works on Conrad in English.] *

17 KEATING, G. T. *A Conrad Memorial Library; the Collection of George T. Keating.* Garden City, N.Y.: Doubleday, 1929.*

18 LOHF, K. A., and E. SHEEHY. *Joseph Conrad at Mid-Century: Editions and Studies 1895-1955.* Minneapolis: U of Minnesota P, 1957. [Not annotated.] *

CRITICAL AND BIOGRAPHICAL BOOKS

1 ALLEN, Jerry. *The Sea Years of Joseph Conrad.* Garden City, N.Y.: Doubleday, 1965.

2 AUBRY, G. J. *The Sea Dreamer; a Definitive Biography of Joseph Conrad.* Trans. Helen Sebba of Aubry's *Vie de Conrad.* Garden City, N.Y.: Doubleday, Page, 1957.

3 BAINES, Jocelyn. *Joseph Conrad.* London: Weidenfeld and Nicolson, 1960. [Now the standard biography.] *†

4 BRADBROOK, M. C. *Joseph Conrad: Poland's English Genius.* New York: Macmillan, 1941.*

5 CONRAD, Jessie. *Joseph Conrad and His Circle.* 2d ed. With a handlist of the various books, pamphlets, prefaces, notes, reviews and letters written about Joseph Conrad, by Richard Curle. Port Washington, N.Y.: Kennikat, 1964.*

6 CRANKSHAW, Edward. *Joseph Conrad; Some Aspects of the Art of the Novel.* New York: Russell and Russell, 1963. [A study of form.]

7 CURLE, R. *The Last Twelve Years of Joseph Conrad.* Garden City, N.Y.: Doubleday, Doran, 1928.

8 FLEISHMAN, Avrom. *Conrad's Politics: Community and Anarchy in the Fiction of Joseph Conrad.* Baltimore: Johns Hopkins, 1967.

9 FOLLETT, Wilson. *Joseph Conrad: A Short Study.* New York: Doubleday, Page, 1915; reissued 1966.

10 FORD, Ford Madox. *Joseph Conrad: A Personal Remembrance.* London: Duckworth, 1924.*

11 GILLON, Adam. *The Eternal Solitary: A Study of Joseph Conrad.* New York: Twayne, 1960.

12 GORDAN, J. D. *Joseph Conrad; the Making of a Novelist.* Cambridge, Mass.: Harvard U P, 1940.*

13 GRAVER, Lawrence. *Conrad's Short Fiction.* Berkeley: U of California P, 1969.

14 GUERARD, A. J. *Conrad the Novelist.* Cambridge, Mass.: Harvard U P, 1958.*

15 GURKO, Leo. *Joseph Conrad: Giant in Exile.* New York: Macmillan, 1962.

16 HAUGH, R. F. *Joseph Conrad: Discovery in Design.* Norman, Okla.: Oklahoma U P, 1957.

17 HAY, Eloise Knapp. *The Political Novels of Joseph Conrad.* Chicago: U of Chicago P, 1963.*

18 HEWITT, D. *Conrad: A Reassessment.* Cambridge: Bowes and Bowes, 1952.*

19 KARL, Frederick. *A Reader's Guide to Joseph Conrad.* New York: Noonday, 1960.*†

1 MEGROZ, R. L. *Joseph Conrad's Mind and Method.* London: Faber and Faber, 1931; 1964.*

2 MEYER, Bernard C. *Joseph Conrad: A Psychoanalytic Biography.* Princeton: Princeton U P, 1967.†

3 MOSER, T. J. *Joseph Conrad: Achievement and Decline.* Cambridge, Mass.: Harvard U P, 1957.*

4 ROSENFIELD, Claire. *Paradise of Snakes: An Archetypal Analysis of Conrad's Political Novels.* Chicago: U of Chicago P, 1967.

5 SAID, Edward. *Joseph Conrad and the Fiction of Autobiography.* Cambridge, Mass.: Harvard U P, 1966.*

6 SELTZER, Leon. *The Vision of Melville and Conrad.* Athens, Ohio: Ohio U P, 1970.

7 SHERRY, Norman. *Conrad's Eastern World.* Cambridge: Cambridge U P, 1966.*

8 STEWART, J. I. M. *Joseph Conrad.* New York: Dodd, Mead, 1968.

9 WARNER, O. *Joseph Conrad.* London: Longmans, Green, 1951.†

10 WILEY, Paul L. *Conrad's Measure of Man.* Madison: U of Wisconsin P, 1954. Repr. New York: Gordian, 1966.*

11 WRIGHT, Walter F. *Romance and Tragedy in Joseph Conrad.* Lincoln, Neb.: U of Nebraska P, 1949.*

CRITICAL ESSAYS

The first seven titles are collections of essays in journals or books.

12 *Conradiana.* Published thrice yearly. College Park, Md.: Department of English, U of Maryland, Spring 1968- .

13 *NRF* 23(1924):645-758. [Pieces by André Gide, Paul Valéry, Edmond Jaloux, André Maurois.]

14 *MFS* 1(1955). Issue devoted to Conrad.

15 "Joseph Conrad Today." *LonM* 4(1957):21-49. [A Centennial symposium. Essays by Oliver Warner, John Wain, W. W. Robson, Richard Freislich, Tom Hopkinson, Jocelyn Baines, Richard Curle.]

16 KRZYZANOWSKI, L., ed. *Joseph Conrad: Centennial Essays.* New York: Polish Institute of Arts and Sciences in America, 1960.

17 MUDRICK, M., ed. *Conrad: A Collection of Critical Essays.* Englewood Cliffs, N.J.: Prentice-Hall, 1966.†

18 STALLMAN, R. W., ed. *The Art of Joseph Conrad: A Critical Symposium.* East Lansing, Mich.: Michigan State U P, 1960. [Contributions by 35 writers, American and European.]

19 BANTOCK, G. H. "Conrad and Politics." *ELH* 25(1958):122-36.

20 BANTOCK, G. H. "The Two 'Moralities' of Joseph Conrad." *EIC* 3(1953): 125-42.

1 BEACH, Joseph Warren. "Impressionism: Conrad." See 11.1, pp. 337-65.*

2 BENSON, C. "Conrad's Two Stories of Initiation." *PMLA* 69(1954):46-56.*

3 BOJARSKI, Edmund A. "Joseph Conrad's Polish Soul." *ES* 44(1963):431-7. [Interview.]

4 BROWN, Douglas. "From *Heart of Darkness* to *Nostromo*: An Approach to Conrad." See 8.3, Ford, pp. 119-37.*

5 BROWN, E. K. "James and Conrad." *YR* 35(1946):265-85.

6 DAICHES, D. See 7.17, pp. 25-62.

7 DANIEL-ROPS, H. "Joseph Conrad." *Carte D'Europe: Strindberg-Conrad-Tchekhov-Unamuno-Pirandello-Duhamel-Rilke.* Paris: Librarie Académique, 1928, pp. 53-84.*

8 DIKE, Donald A. "The Tempest of Axel Heyst." *NCF* 17(1962):95-113.

9 FEDER, Lillian. "Marlow's Descent into Hell." *NCF* 9(1955):280-92. Repr. in 27.18, pp. 162-70.

10 FERNANDEZ, R. "The Art of Conrad." *Messages.* New York: Harcourt, Brace, 1927, pp. 137-51. Repr. in 27.18, pp. 8-13.*

11 FLEISCHMANN, Wolfgang B. "Conrad's *Chance* and Bergson's *Laughter.*" *Ren* 14(1960-62):66-71.

12 FORD, Ford Madox. "Conrad and the Sea." See 37.17, pp. 76-92.

13 FORSTER, E. M. "Joseph Conrad: A Note." *Abinger Harvest.* New York: Harcourt, Brace, 1936, pp. 130-4.

14 GATCH, Katherine H. "Conrad's Axel." *SP* 48(1951):98-106.

15 GOETSCH, Paul. "Joseph Conrad: *Nostromo.*" See 16.9, Oppel, pp. 49-77.

16 GOLDKNOPF, David. "What's Wrong with Conrad: Conrad on Conrad." *Criticism* 10(1968):54-64.

17 GOSE, Elliott B., Jr. "Pure Exercise of Imagination: Archetypal Symbolism in *Lord Jim.*" *PMLA* 79(1964):137-47.

18 GROSS, Harvey. "Aschenbach and Kurtz: The Cost of Civilization." *Centennial Review* 6(1962):131-43.

19 GUETTI, James. "Heart of Darkness: The Failure of Imagination." *The Limits of Metaphor: A Study of Melville, Conrad, and Faulkner.* Ithaca, N.Y.: Cornell U P, 1967, pp. 46-68.

20 HAGAN, John H., Jr. "The Design of Conrad's *The Secret Agent.*" *ELH* 22(1955):148-64.

21 HALVERSON, J., and Ian WATT. "The Original Nostromo." *RES* 10(1959):45-52.

22 HEDSPETH, Robert N. "Conrad's Use of Time in *Chance.*" *NCF* 21(1966-1967):283-9.

1 HERNDON, Richard. "The Genesis of Conrad's 'Amy Foster.'" *SP* 57(1960):549-66.

2 HOARE, Dorothy M. "The Tragic in Hardy and Conrad." See 16.4, pp. 113-32.

3 HOUGH, Graham. "*Chance* and Joseph Conrad." *Image and Experience: Studies in a Literary Revolution.* London: Duckworth, 1960, pp. 211-22.*

4 HOWE, Irving. "Conrad: Order and Anarchy." See 14.7, pp. 76-113.

5 JAMES, Henry. See 8.10, pp. 345-53. [Conrad's *Chance.*]

6 JOHNSON, Bruce. "Conrad's 'Falk': Manuscript and Meaning." *MLQ* 26(1965):267-84.

7 KAEHELE, Sharon, and Howard GERMAN. "Conrad's *Victory*: A Reassessment." *MFS* 10(1964):55-72.

8 KAPLAN, Harold. "Character as Reality: Joseph Conrad." *The Passive Voice: An Approach to Modern Fiction.* Athens, Ohio: Ohio U P, 1966, pp. 131-57.

9 KERF, René. "*The Nigger of the 'Narcissus'* and the Ms. Version of *The Rescue.*" *ES* 44(1963):437-43.

10 KETTLE, Arnold. "Joseph Conrad: *Nostromo.*" See 16.7, II, pp. 67-81.

11 KIRSCHNER, Paul. "Conrad and Maupassant." *REL* 6(1965):37-51.

12 KIRSCHNER, Paul. "Conrad and Maupassant: Moral Solitude and 'A Smile of Fortune.'" *REL* 7(1966):62-77.*

13 KNOPF, A. A. "Joseph Conrad: A Footnote to Publishing History." *Atlantic Monthly* 201(1958):63-7.

14 KRAMER, Dale. "Marlow, Myth, and Structure in *Lord Jim.*" *Criticism* 8(1966):263-79.

15 KRIEGER, Murray. "Joseph Conrad: Action, Inaction, and Extremity." See 14.11, pp. 154-65.

16 KRZYZANOWSKI, L. "Joseph Conrad: Some Polish Documents." *PolR* 3(1958):59-85.

17 LEAVIS, F. R. "Joseph Conrad." *SR* 66(1958):179-200.

18 LEAVIS, F. R. See 10.2, pp. 192-248.*

19 LEHMANN, John. "On Re-reading *The Rover.*" *The Open Night.* London: Longmans, Green, 1952, pp. 54-62.

20 LEWIS, R. W. B. "The Current of Conrad's *Victory.*" *Twelve Original Essays on Great English Novels.* Ed. Charles Shapiro. Detroit: Wayne State U P, 1960, pp. 203-31.

21 MAC CARTHY, Desmond. "Conrad." *Portraits.* London: Saunders with MacGibbon and Kee, 1955, pp. 68-78.

1 MC CONNELL, Daniel J. " 'The Heart of Darkness' in T. S. Eliot's *The Hollow Men.*" *TSLL* 4(1962):141-53.

2 MANN, Thomas. "Joseph Conrad's *The Secret Agent.*" *Past Masters and Other Papers.* London: Secker, 1933, pp. 231-47. Repr. in 27.18, pp. 227-34.*

3 MILLER, J. Hillis. "Joseph Conrad: I The Darkness; II The Secret Agent." *Poets of Reality: Six Twentieth Century Writers.* New York: Atheneum, 1969.

4 MOORE, Carlisle. "Conrad and the Novel as Ordeal." *PQ* 42(1963):55-74.

5 MORGAN, Gerald. "Conrad, Madach et Calderoni." *ESl* 6(1961):196-209.

6 MOYNIHAN, W. T. "Conrad's 'The End of the Tether': A New Reading." *MFS* 4(1958):173-7. Repr. in 27.18, pp. 186-96.

7 MUDRICK, M. "Conrad and the Terms of Modern Criticism." *HudR* 7(1954):419-26.

8 MUDRICK, M. "The Originality of Conrad." *HudR* 11(1958):545-53. Repr. in 27.17, pp. 37-44.

9 OBER, Warren V. "*Heart of Darkness:* 'The Ancient Mariner' a Hundred Years Later." *DR* 46(1965):333-7.

10 PETERKIEWICZ, Jerzy. "Patriotic Irritability: Conrad and Poland: For the Centenary." *TC* 162(1957):545-57.

11 PRITCHETT, V. S. "Conrad." See 16.11, pp. 190-9.

12 ROBERTSON, J. M. "The Novels of Joseph Conrad." *North American Review* 208(1918):439-53.

13 SAID, Edward. "Conrad, *Nostromo*: Record and Reality." *Approaches to the Twentieth Century Novel.* Ed. John Unterecker. New York: Crowell, 1965, pp. 108-52.

14 SANDISON, Alan. "Joseph Conrad: A Window on to Chaos." *The Wheel of Empire: A Study of the Imperial Idea in Some Late Nineteenth- and Early Twentieth-Century Fiction.* London: Macmillan, 1967, pp. 120-48.

15 SCHWAB, Arnold. "Conrad's American Speeches and His Reading from *Victory.*" *MP* 62(1965):342-7.

16 SCRIMGEOUR, Cecil. "Jimmy Wait and the Dance of Death: Conrad's *Nigger of the 'Narcissus.'* " *CritQ* 7(1965):339-52.*

17 SIMON, Irène. "Joseph Conrad." See 12.19, pp. 258-97.

18 SPECTOR, Robert D. "Irony as Theme: Conrad's *The Secret Agent.*" *NCF* 13(1958):69-71.

19 STALLMAN, Robert W. "The Structure and Symbolism of Conrad's *Victory.*" *Western Review* 13(1949):146-57.

20 STALLMAN, Robert W. "Time and *The Secret Agent.*" *TSLL* 1(1959): 101-22. Repr. in 27.18, pp. 234-54.

1 STEIN, William Bysshe. "Conrad's East: Time, History, Action, and *Maya.*" *TSLL* 7(1965):265-83.

2 STEWART, J. I. M. See 6.4, Chap. V, pp. 184-222 and "Selected Bibliography," pp. 656-65.

3 TANNER, Tony. "Nightmare and Complacency: Razumov and the Western Eye." *CritQ* 4(1962):197-215.

4 THALE, Jerome. "Marlow's Quest." *UTQ* 24(1955):351-8. Repr. in 27.18, pp. 154-62.

5 THALE, Jerome. "The Narrator as Hero." *TCL* 3(1957):69-73.

6 TILLYARD, E. M. W. "Conrad: *Nostromo.*" See 12.21, pp. 126-67.*

7 TILLYARD, E. M. W. "*The Secret Agent* Reconsidered." *EIC* 11(1961): 309-18. Repr. in 27.17, pp. 103-10.*

8 TINDALL, William York. "Apology for Marlow." *From Jane Austen to Joseph Conrad.* Ed. Robert C. Rathburn and Martin Steinmann, Jr. Minneapolis: U of Minnesota P, 1958, pp. 274-85.

9 TOLIVER, Harold E. "Conrad's *Arrow of Gold* and Pastoral Tradition." *MFS* 8(1962):148-58.

10 URE, P. "Character and Imagination in Conrad." *Cambridge Journal* 3(1950):727-40.

11 VAN GHENT, Dorothy. "On *Lord Jim.*" See 10.17, pp. 229-44. Repr. in 27.18, pp. 142-53.

12 VIDAN, I. "One Source of Conrad's *Nostromo.*" *RES* 7(1956):287-93.

13 WARREN, Robert Penn. See 25.3, pp. vii-xxxix. Repr. in 27.18, pp. 209-27.*

14 WATT, Ian. "Joseph Conrad: Alientation and Commitment." *The English Mind: Studies in the English Moralists Presented to Basil Wiley.* Ed. Hugh Sykes Davies and George Watson. Cambridge: Cambridge U P, 1964, pp. 257-78.

15 WATT, Ian. "Story and Idea in Conrad's 'The Shadow Line.'" *CritQ* 2(1960):133-48.*

16 WATTS, C. T. "Joseph Conrad and the Ranee of Sarawak." *RES* 15(1964): 404-7.

17 WEBSTER, H. T. "Conrad's Changes in Narrative Conception in the Manuscripts of *Typhoon and Other Stories* and *Victory.*" *PMLA* 64(1949): 953-62.*

18 WILDING, Michael. "The Politics of *Nostromo.*" *EIC* 16(1966):441-56.*

19 WILEY, Paul L. "Conrad's Skein of Ironies." See 25.6, pp. 223-7.

20 WOOLF, Virginia. "Joseph Conrad." See 114.15, I, pp. 302-18.

1 WOOLF, Virginia. "Mr. Conrad: A Conversation." See 114.15, I, pp. 309-13.

2 WRIGHT, Elizabeth Cox. "The Defining Function of Vocabulary in Conrad's *The Rover.*" *SAQ* 59(1960):265-77.*

3 WRIGHT, Walter F. "Joseph Conrad's Critical Views." *Research Studies of the State College of Washington* 12(1944):155-75.

4 YOUNG, V. "Lingard's Folly: The Lost Subject." *KR* 15(1953):522-39. Repr. in 27.18, pp. 96-108.*

5 ZABEL, Morton Dauwen. "Conrad." See 16.19, pp. 147-227.*

6 ZABEL, Morton Dauwen. "Introduction." See 25.5, pp. 1-47.

7 ZABEL, Morton Dauwen. "Introduction." See 25.4, pp. ix-lviii. Repr. in 27.17, pp. 111-44.*

Norman Douglas (1868-1952)

TEXTS

There is no collected edition.

8 *South Wind.* London: Secker, 1917. Rev. with introduction by William King. London: Secker and Warburg, 1946.

9 *South Wind.* With new introduction by Douglas, pp. v-vii. New York: Modern Library, 1925.

10 *Old Calabria.* Introduction by Douglas, pp. vi-viii. London: Oxford U P, 1938. [Distinguished nonfictional prose work.] †

11 *Old Calabria.* Introduction by John Davenport. New York: Harcourt, Brace, 1956.

12 *Late Harvest.* London: Drummond, 1946. [Reminiscences by Douglas with comments on his books.]

13 *Looking Back: An Autobiographical Excursion.* London: Chatto and Windus; New York: Harcourt, Brace, 1933.

14 *Norman Douglas: A Selection from His Works with an Introduction by D. M. Low.* London: Chatto and Windus with Secker and Warburg, 1955. [Selections from *South Wind*, travel books, essays, autobiographies, and other prose.] *

BIBLIOGRAPHIES

15 MC DONALD, Edward D. *A Bibliography of Norman Douglas.* Philadelphia: Centaur Book Shop, 1927. [Includes notes by Douglas.] *

16 WOOLF, Cecil. *A Bibliography of Norman Douglas.* London: Hart-Davis, 1954.*

CRITICAL AND BIOGRAPHICAL BOOKS

1 ALDINGTON, Richard. *Pinorman: Personal Recollections of Norman Douglas. Pino Orioli, and Charles Prentice.* London: Heinemann, 1954.

2 CUNARD, Nancy. *Grand Man: Memories of Norman Douglas.* London: Secker and Warburg, 1954.

3 DAWKINS, R. M. *Norman Douglas.* London: Hart-Davis, 1952.*†

4 FITZGIBBON, Constantine. *Norman Douglas: A Pictorial Record.* London: Richards, 1953. [Includes a critical and biographical study.]

5 GREENLEES, Ian. *Norman Douglas.* London: Longmans, Green, 1957. [British Council pamphlet.]

6 LINDEMAN, Ralph D. *Norman Douglas.* New York: Twayne, 1965. [Annotated bibliography.]

7 TOMLINSON, H. M. *Norman Douglas.* London: Hutchinson, 1952.

CRITICAL ESSAYS

8 AUBRY, G. J. See 25.9, II, pp. 23, 24, 67-9, 99-100, 113. [Conrad-Douglas letters.]

9 DAVENPORT, John. "Norman Douglas." *TC* 151(1952):359-67.

10 ECKERSLEY, Arthur. "The Work of Mr. Norman Douglas." *Anglo-Italian Review* 3(1919):40-4.

11 FLINT, R. W. "Norman Douglas." *KR* 14(1952):660-8.

12 GREENE, Graham. "Norman Douglas." See 54.8, pp. 362-5.

13 HUEFFER [FORD], Ford Madox. "A Haughty and Proud Generation." *YR* 11(1922):703-17. [Places Douglas with other contemporaries.]

14 LOW, D. M. "Introduction." See 32.14, pp. 9-24.*

15 MC DONALD, Edward D. "The Early Works of Norman Douglas." *Bookman* (American) 66(1927):42-6.

16 PRITCHETT, V. S. *New Statesman and Nation* 43(1952):307-8.

17 WEBSTER, H. T. "Norman Douglas: A Reconsideration." *SAQ* 49(1950):226-36.*

18 WHEATLEY, Elizabeth D. "Norman Douglas." *SR* 40(1932):55-67.

19 WILSON, Edmund. "The Nietzchean Line." See 6.15, pp. 485-91.

Lawrence Durrell (1912-)

TEXTS

1 *The Alexandria Quartet: Justine, Balthazar, Mountolive, Clea.* London: Faber and Faber; New York: Dutton, 1962.*†

2 *The Black Book: An Agon.* Paris: Obelisk, 1938. [No. 1 of the Villa Seurat Series, ed. by Henry Miller.] *

3 *The Black Book: An Agon.* Introduction by Gerald Sikes. New York: Dutton, 1960.†

4 Introduction to Georg Groddeck, *The Book of the It.* New York: Vintage Books, 1961, pp. v-xxiv. [Originally published as "Studies in Genius," No. VI. *Horizon* 17(1948):384-403. Important for Durrell's literary theory.] †

5 *A Key to Modern British Poetry.* Norman, Okla.: U of Oklahoma P, 1952. Under title *Key to Modern Poetry.* London: Nevill, 1952. [Contains ideas pertinent to *The Alexandria Quartet.*] *†

6 *Lawrence Durrell and Henry Miller: A Private Correspondence.* Ed. George Wickes. New York: Dutton; London: Faber and Faber, 1963. [Of biographical importance.] *†

7 "Lawrence Durrell." See 6.16, Second Series, pp. 257-82. [Interview.]

8 YOUNG, Kenneth. "A Dialogue with Durrell." *Encounter* 13(1959):61-8. [Interview.]

BIBLIOGRAPHIES

9 POTTER, Robert A., and Brooke WHITING. *Lawrence Durrell: A Checklist.* Preface by Lawrence Clark Powell. Los Angeles: U of California Library, 1961.

10 THOMAS, Alan G. "Bibliography." In 34.11, pp. 200-50. [Includes critical studies of Durrell.] *

CRITICAL AND BIOGRAPHICAL BOOKS

11 FRASER, G. S. *Lawrence Durrell: A Critical Study.* London: Faber and Faber, 1968.*

12 PERLES, Alfred. *My Friend Lawrence Durrell.* Northwood, Middlesex: Scorpion, 1961. [Bibliography by Bernard Stone included.]

13 UNTERECKER, John. *Lawrence Durrell.* New York: Columbia U P, 1964. [Columbia Essays on Modern Writers.]

1 WEIGEL, John A. *Lawrence Durrell.* New York: Twayne, 1965. [Includes selected bibliography.]

CRITICAL ESSAYS
The first title is a collection.

2 MOORE, Harry T., ed. *The World of Lawrence Durrell.* Carbondale, Ill.: Southern Illinois U P, 1962. [Essays by 17 writers.] *

3 ARBAN, Dominique. "Lawrence Durrell." *Preuves* 109(1960):86-94.

4 ARTHOS, John. "Lawrence Durrell's Gnosticism." *Person* 43(1961):360-73.

5 BODE, Carl. "Durrell's Way to Alexandria." *CE* 22(1961):531-8.

6 CORKE, Hilary. "Mr. Durrell and Brother Criticus." *Encounter* 14(1960): 65-70. *[Alexandria Quartet.]*

7 DE MOTT, Benjamin. "Grading the Emanglons." *HudR* 13(1960):457-64. [*Alexandria Quartet.*]

8 HAMARD, J.-P. "L'espace et le temps dans les romans de Lawrence Durrell." *Critique* (Paris) No. 156(1960):387-413.*

9 HAMARD, J.-P. "Lawrence Durrell, rénovateur assagi." *Critique* (Paris) No. 163(1960):1025-33.

10 HOWARTH, Herbert. "A Segment of Durrell's Alexandria Quartet." *UTQ* 32(1963):282-93.

11 KARL, Frederick. "Lawrence Durrell: Physical and Metaphysical Love." See 16.5, pp. 40-61.

12 KERMODE, Frank. "Durrell and Others." See 16.6, pp. 214-27.

13 O'BRIEN, R. A. "Time, Space and Language in Lawrence Durrell." *Waterloo Review* 6(1961):16-24.

14 PROSER, Matthew N. "Darley's Dilemma: The Problem of Structure in Durrell's *Alexandria Quartet.*" *Crit* 4(1961):18-28.

15 REXROTH, Kenneth. "Lawrence Durrell." *Assays.* Norfolk, Conn.: New Directions, 1961, pp. 118-30.

16 RIPPIER, Joseph S. "Lawrence Durrell." See 16.13, pp. 106-37.

17 ROMBERG, Bertil. *"The Alexandria Quartet."* See 12.17, pp. 277-308.*

18 WEATHERHEAD, A. K. "Romantic Anachronism in *The Alexandria Quartet.*" *MFS* 10(1964):128-36.

36

Ronald Firbank (1886-1926)

TEXTS

1 *The Works of Ronald Firbank.* Introduction by Arthur Waley and a biographical memoir by Sir Osbert Sitwell. 5 vols. London: Duckworth; New York: Brentano's, 1929. [In 1934, 6 vols. by addition of *The Artificial Princess.*]

2 *The Works of Ronald Firbank.* Omnibus Edition. 2 vols. Vol. I: *Five Novels.* Introduction by Sir Osbert Sitwell. Portrait by Augustus John. Vol. II: *Three Novels.* Introduction by Ernest Jones. London: Duckworth, 1949-1950; Norfolk, Conn.: New Directions, 1949-1950.

3 *The Complete Ronald Firbank.* Preface by Anthony Powell. 1 vol. London: Duckworth; Norfolk: New Directions, 1961.

4 *Ronald Firbank Two Novels: The Flower Beneath the Foot; Prancing Nigger.* With a chronology by M. J. Benkovitz. Norfolk, Conn.: New Directions, 1962.†

5 *The New Rhythm and Other Pieces.* Introduction by Alan Harris. London: Duckworth, 1962. Norfolk, Conn.: New Directions, 1964. [Contains an unfinished novel with American background.]

BIBLIOGRAPHIES

6 BENKOVITZ, M. J. *Ronald Firbank: A Bibliography.* London: Hart-Davis, 1963.*

CRITICAL AND BIOGRAPHICAL BOOKS

7 BENKOVITZ, M. J. *Ronald Firbank.* New York: Knopf, 1969.*

8 BROOKE, Jocelyn. *Ronald Firbank.* New York: Roy, 1951.

9 BROOKE, Jocelyn. "Ronald Firbank." *Ronald Firbank and John Betjeman.* London: Longmans, Green, 1962, pp. 5-24. [British Council pamphlet.]

10 FLETCHER, I. K. *Ronald Firbank: A Memoir.* London: Duckworth, 1930.

CRITICAL ESSAYS

11 AUDEN, W. H. "Ronald Firbank and an Amateur World." *Listener* 65(1961):1004-5, 1008.

12 BENKOVITZ, M. J. "Ronald Firbank in New York." *BNYPL* (May 1959): 247-59.

13 BRAYBROOKE, Neville. "Ronald Firbank, 1886-1926." *DR* 42(1962-1963):38-49.

14 CONNOLLY, Cyril. See 11.8, pp. 45-51.

1 FORSTER, E. M. "Ronald Firbank." See 28.13, pp. 115-21.

2 HAFLEY, James. "Ronald Firbank." *ArQ* 12(1966):161-71.*

3 HARRIS, Alan. "Introduction." See 36.5, pp. 9-17.

4 JONES, Ernest. "Introduction." See 36.2, II, pp. xii-xx.

5 POWELL, Anthony. "Preface." See 36.3, pp. 5-16.

6 PRITCHETT, V. S. "Firbank." *Books in General.* London: Chatto and Windus, 1953, pp. 229-34.

7 SITWELL, Sir Osbert. "Ronald Firbank." *Noble Essences: A Book of Characters.* Boston: Little, Brown, 1950, pp. 77-100.*

8 WALEY, Arthur. "Introduction." See 36.1, I, pp. 2-11.

9 WAUGH, Evelyn. "Ronald Firbank." *Life and Letters* 2(1929):191-6.*

10 WILSON, Edmund. "A Revival of Ronald Firbank." See 6.14, pp. 486-502.*

Ford Madox Ford (1873-1939)

TEXTS

11 *The Bodley Head Ford Madox Ford.* Ed. and with introduction by Graham Greene. 4 vols. London: Bodley Head, 1962-1963. *The Good Soldier*, Selected Memories, Poems, *The Fifth Queen* trilogy [*The Fifth Queen, Privy Seal, The Fifth Queen Crowned*], and *Parade's End.*

12 *The Good Soldier: A Tale of Passion.* London: Lane, 1915. New ed. with introduction by Mark Schorer and Ford's "Dedicatory Letter to Stella Ford." New York: Knopf, 1951.†

13 *Some Do Not. No More Parades. A Man Could Stand Up. Last Post.* Preface by R. A. Scott-James. West Drayton, Middlesex: Penguin, 1948.

14 *Parade's End.* Introduction by Robie Macauley. New York: Knopf, 1950.

15 *Parade's End.* Afterword to each volume by Arthur Mizener. 2 vols. Vol. 1: *Some Do Not* and *No More Parades.* Vol. 2: *A Man Could Stand Up* and *Last Post.* New York: Signet Classics, 1964. [Reprinted from the English first editions.] †

16 *The Fifth Queen Trilogy.* [*The Fifth Queen, Privy Seal, The Fifth Queen Crowned.*] New York: Vanguard, 1964.

17 *Portraits from Life: Memories and Criticisms.* Boston: Houghton Mifflin, 1937. [Published in England as *Mightier Than the Sword.* London: Allen and Unwin, 1938.] †

18 *Letters of Ford Madox Ford.* Ed. Richard M. Ludwig. Princeton: Princeton U P, 1965.*

19 *Critical Writings of Ford Madox Ford.* Ed. Frank MacShane. Lincoln, Neb.: U of Nebraska P, 1964.*†

BIBLIOGRAPHIES

1 BEEBE, Maurice, and Robert G. JOHNSON. "Criticism of Ford Madox Ford: A Selected Checklist." *MFS* 9(1963):94-100.*

2 GERBER, Helmut E., ed. "Ford Madox Ford: An Annotated Checklist." *EFT* 1(1958):2-19; 4(1961):11-29.

3 HARVEY, David Dow. *Ford Madox Ford 1873-1939: A Bibliography of Works and Criticism.* Princeton: Princeton U P, 1962.*

4 NAUMBURG, Edward, Jr. "A Catalogue of a Ford Madox Ford Collection." *PULC* 9(1948):134-65.

CRITICAL AND BIOGRAPHICAL BOOKS

5 BOWEN, Stella. *Drawn From Life.* London: Collins, 1941. [Biographical.]

6 CASSELL, Richard A. *Ford Madox Ford: A Study of His Novels.* Baltimore: Johns Hopkins, 1961.*

7 GOLDRING, Douglas. *South Lodge: Reminiscences of Violet Hunt, Ford Madox Ford, and the English Review Circle.* London: Constable, 1943.

8 GOLDRING, Douglas. *Trained for Genius.* New York: Dutton, 1949. [Published as *The Last Pre-Raphaelite.* London: MacDonald, 1948. Biographical but not definitive.]

9 GORDON, Ambrose, Jr. *The Invisible Tent: The War Novels of Ford Madox Ford.* Austin: U of Texas P, 1964.

10 GORDON, Caroline. *A Good Soldier: A Key to the Novels of Ford Madox Ford.* Davis, Calif.: U of California Library, 1963. [Chapbook No. 1.]

11 HOFFMANN, Charles G. *Ford Madox Ford.* New York: Twayne, 1967.

12 HUNT, Violet. *I Have This to Say.* New York: Boni and Liveright, 1926, *passim.* [Published as *The Flurried Years.* London: Hurst and Blackett, 1926.] *

13 HUNTLEY, H. Robert. *The Alien Protagonist of Ford Madox Ford.* Chapel Hill: U of North Carolina P, 1970.

14 LID, Richard W. *Ford Madox Ford: The Essence of His Art.* Berkeley: U of California P, 1964.

15 MAC SHANE, Frank. *The Life and Works of Ford Madox Ford.* New York: Horizon, 1965. [Biographical.] *

16 MEIXNER, John A. *Ford Madox Ford's Novels: A Critical Study.* Minneapolis: U of Minnesota P, 1962.*

17 MIZENER, Arthur. *The Saddest Story: A Biography of Ford Madox Ford.* New York: World, 1971.*

18 OHMANN, Carol. *Ford Madox Ford: From Apprentice to Craftsman.* Middletown, Conn.: Wesleyan U P, 1964.

1 POLI, Bernard. *Ford Madox Ford and the Transatlantic Review.* Syracuse: Syracuse U P, 1967.*

2 WILEY, Paul L. *Novelist of Three Worlds: Ford Madox Ford.* Syracuse: Syracuse U P, 1962.*

3 YOUNG, Kenneth. *Ford Madox Ford.* London: Longmans, Green, 1956. [British Council pamphlet.]

CRITICAL ESSAYS
The first two titles are collections.

4 *New Directions: Number 7.* Norfolk, Conn.: New Directions, 1942. [Reminiscences and appraisals, including Aldington, Pound, Caroline Gordon, William Carlos Williams, Granville Hicks.]

5 *MFS* 9(Spring, 1963). Issue devoted to Ford.

6 ALDINGTON, Richard. *Life for Life's Sake: A Book of Reminiscences.* New York: Viking, 1941, pp. 149-59.

7 BAINES, Jocelyn. See 26.3, pp. 216-23 and *passim.* [Account of the Ford-Conrad collaboration.] *

8 BENDER, Todd K. "The Sad Tale of Dowell: Ford Madox Ford's *The Good Soldier.*" *Criticism* 4(1962):353-68.

9 BLACKMUR, R. P. "The King over the Water: Notes on the Novels of F. M. Hueffer." *PULC* 9(1948):123-7.

10 CONRAD, Jessie. See 26.5, *passim.*

11 COX, James T. "Ford's 'Passion for Provence.' " *ELH* 28(1961):383-98.

12 CRANKSHAW, Edward. See 26.6, *passim.*

13 CRANKSHAW, Edward. "Ford Madox Ford." *National Review* 131(1948): 160-7.

14 GOSE, Elliott B. "The Strange Irregular Rhythm: An Analysis of *The Good Soldier.*" *PMLA* 72(1957):494-509.*

15 GREENE, Graham. "Ford Madox Ford." See 54.8, pp. 159-71.

16 HARVEY, David Dow. "Pro Patria Mori: The Neglect of Ford's Novels in England." *MFS* 9(1963):3-16.

17 HOFFMANN, Charles G. "Ford's Manuscript Revisions of *The Good Soldier.*" *ELT* 9(1966):145-52.*

18 HYNES, Samuel. "Ford and the Spirit of Romance." *MFS* 9(1963):17-24.

19 KENNER, Hugh. *The Poetry of Ezra Pound.* Norfolk, Conn.: New Directions, 1968, pp. 258-9, 264-72.

20 LEHAN, Richard. "Ford Madox Ford and the Absurd: *The Good Soldier.*" *TSLL* 5(1963):219-31.

21 LUDWIG, Richard M. "The Reputation of Ford Madox Ford." *PMLA* 76(1961):544-51.*

22 MACAULEY, Robie. "The Good Ford." *KR* 11(1949):269-88.*

1 MC FATE, Patricia, and Bruce GOLDEN. *"The Good Soldier;* a Tragedy of Self-Deception." *MFS* 9(1963):50-60.

2 MAC SHANE, Frank. "A Conscious Craftsman: Ford Madox Ford's Manuscript Revisions." *Boston University Studies in English* 5(1961):178-84.*

3 MAC SHANE, Frank. "Ford Madox Ford and His Contemporaries: Techniques of the Novel." *ELT* 4(1961):2-11.

4 MIZENER, Arthur. "Afterword." See 37.15, I, pp. 505-17; II, pp. 337-50.*

5 PRITCHETT, V. S. "Fordie." See 16.11, pp. 251-63.

6 SCHORER, Mark. "An Interpretation." See 37.12, pp. v-xv. [Published originally in *PULC* 9(1948):128-33.] *

7 WAGNER, Geoffrey. "Ford Madox Ford: The Honest Edwardian." *EIC* 17(1967):75-88.

8 WALTER, E. V. "The Political Sense of Ford Madox Ford." *New Republic* 134(1956):17-9.

9 ZABEL, Morton Dauwen. "Yesterday and After." See 16.19, pp. 253-63.

E. M. Forster (1879-1970)

TEXTS

10 *The Works of E. M. Forster.* Pocket Edition. London: Arnold, 1947- . (Includes five novels and *Aspects of the Novel, Abinger Harvest,* and *Goldsworthy Lowes Dickinson.*]

11 *A Passage to India.* New York: Modern Library, 1940. [Repr. from 1st American ed. New York: Harcourt, Brace, 1934.]

12 *A Passage to India.* Introduction by Peter Burra. Foreword and author's notes by Forster. London: Dent, 1942.*†

13 *The Longest Journey.* Introduction by Forster. London: Oxford U P, 1960.†

14 "Arctic Summer." *Tribute to Benjamin Britten on His Fiftieth Birthday.* Ed. Anthony Gishford. London: Faber and Faber, 1963, pp. 46-55. [Section of unfinished novel.]

BIBLIOGRAPHIES

15 BEEBE, Maurice, and Joseph BROGUNIER. "Criticism of E. M. Forster: A Selected Checklist." *MFS* 7(1961):284-92.

16 GERBER, Helmut E. "E. M. Forster: An Annotated Checklist of Writings About Him." *ELT* 2(1959):4-27. [This is being kept up to date in *ELT*.] *

1 KIRKPATRICK, B. J. *A Bibliography of E. M. Forster.* London: Hart-Davis, 1965; 2d ed., 1968.†

CRITICAL AND BIOGRAPHICAL BOOKS

2 BEER, J. B. *The Achievement of E. M. Forster.* London: Chatto and Windus, 1962.*

3 BRANDER, L. *E. M. Forster: A Critical Study.* London: Hart-Davis, 1968.

4 CREWS, F. C. *E. M. Forster: The Perils of Humanism.* Princeton: Princeton U P, 1962.*†

5 GRANSDEN, K. W. *E. M. Forster.* New York: Grove, 1962.

6 KELVIN, Norman. *E. M. Forster.* Carbondale, Ill.: Southern Illinois U P, 1967.

7 MACAULAY, Rose. *The Writings of E. M. Forster.* London: Hogarth, 1938.

8 MC CONKEY, James. *The Novels of E. M. Forster.* Ithaca, N.Y.: Cornell U P, 1957.

9 NATWAR-SINGH, K., ed. *E. M. Forster: A Tribute.* New York: Harcourt, Brace and World, 1964.

10 SHUSTERMAN, David. *The Quest for Certitude in E. M. Forster's Fiction.* Bloomington: Indiana U P, 1966.

11 STONE, Wilfred. *The Cave and the Mountain: A Study of E. M. Forster.* Stanford: Stanford U P, 1966.*†

12 THOMSON, George H. *The Fiction of E. M. Forster.* Detroit: Wayne State U P, 1967.

13 TRILLING, Lionel. *E. M. Forster.* London: Hogarth, 1967.*†

14 WILDE, Alan. *Art and Order: A Study of E. M. Forster.* New York: New York U P, 1964.*

CRITICAL ESSAYS
The first four titles are collections.

15 BRADBURY, Malcolm, ed. *Forster: A Collection of Critical Essays.* Englewood Cliffs, N.J.: Prentice-Hall, 1968.*

16 *MFS* 7(Autumn 1961). E. M. Forster Number.

17 SHAHANE, V. A., ed. *Perspectives on E. M. Forster's "A Passage to India": A Collection of Critical Essays.* New York: Barnes and Noble, 1968.

18 STALLYBRASS, Oliver, ed. *Aspects of E. M. Forster: Essays and Recollections Written for His Ninetieth Birthday, January 1, 1969.* New York: Harcourt, Brace and World, 1969.

1 ALLEN, Glen O. "Structure, Symbol, and Theme in E. M. Forster's *A Passage to India.*" *PMLA* 70(1955):934-54. Repr. in 41.17.

2 BEAUMONT, Ernest. "Mr. E. M. Forster's Strange Mystics." *Dublin Review* 225(1951):41-51.

3 BOWEN, Elizabeth. "E. M. Forster, I-II." See 19.9, pp. 119-26.

4 BRADBURY, Malcolm. "E. M. Forster's *Howards End.*" *CritQ* 4(1962): 229-41. Repr. in 41.15.*

5 BROWER, Reuben A. "Beyond E. M. Forster: Part 1–The Earth." *Foreground* 1(1946):164-74.

6 BROWER, Reuben A. "Beyond E. M. Forster: The Unseen." *ChiR* 2(1948): 102-12.

7 BROWER, Reuben A. "The Twilight of the Double Vision: Symbol and Irony in *A Passage to India.*" Chap. 10 of *The Fields of Light: An Experience in Critical Reading.* New York: Oxford U P, 1951.*

8 BROWN, E. K. "Rhythm in E. M. Forster's *A Passage to India.*" See 11.4, pp. 46-55, 89-115.

9 BURRA, Peter. "Introduction." See 40.12, pp. xi-xxviii. Repr. in 41.15.*

10 CECIL, Lord David. "E. M. Forster." *Poets and Story Tellers: A Book of Critical Essays.* London: Constable, 1968, pp. 181-201.

11 CHURCHILL, Thomas. "Place and Personality in *Howards End.*" *Crit* 5(1962):61-73.

12 CREWS, F. C. "E. M. Forster: The Limitations of Mythology." *CL* 12(1960):97-112. Repr. in 41.15.*

13 DALESKI, H. M. "Rhythmic and Symbolic Patterns in *A Passage to India.*" *Studies in English Language and Literature.* Ed. Alice Shalvi and A. A. Mendilow. Jerusalem: The Hebrew University, 1966, pp. 258-79.

14 DOBREE, Bonamy. "E. M. Forster." *The Lamp and the Lute: Studies in Six Modern Authors.* 2d ed. London: Cass, 1964, pp. 65-81.

15 FURBANK, P. N., and F. J. H. HASKELL. "E. M. Forster." See 6.16, First Series, pp. 23-35.

16 FUSSELL, Paul, Jr. "E. M. Forster's Mrs. Moore: Some Suggestions." *PQ* 32(1953):388-95.

17 HALL, James. "Family Reunions: E. M. Forster." See 16.2, pp. 11-30.

18 HANNAH, Donald. "The Limitations of Liberalism in E. M. Forster's Work." *EM* 13(1962):165-78.

19 HARVEY, John. "Imagination and Moral Theme in E. M. Forster's *The Longest Journey.*" *EIC* 6(1956):418-33. Repr. in 41.15.

20 HOARE, Dorothy M. "E. M. Forster." See 16.4, pp. 68-97.

1 HOFFMAN, F. J. "*Howards End* and the Bogey of Progress." *MFS* 7(1961): 243-57.

2 HOLLINGSWORTH, Keith. "*A Passage to India:* The Echoes in the Marabar Caves." *Criticism* 4(1962):210-24. Repr. in 41.17.

3 HOLT, Lee Elbert. "E. M. Forster and Samuel Butler." *PMLA* 61(1946): 804-19.*

4 HOY, Cyrus. "Forster's Metaphysical Novel." *PMLA* 75(1960):126-36. [*Howards End.*] *

5 JOHNSTONE, J. K. "E. M. Forster." See 5.6, pp. 159-266.

6 KERMODE, Frank. "Mr. E. M. Forster as a Symbolist." *Listener* 59(January 2, 1958):17-8. Repr. in 41.15.

7 KETTLE, Arnold. "E. M. Forster: A Passage to India." See 16.7, II, pp. 152-63.

8 KLINGOPULOS, G. D. "E. M. Forster's Sense of History: and Cavafy." *EIC* 8(1958):156-65.*

9 LAWRENCE, D. H. See 72.15, I and II, pp. 315, 316, 317-8, 323, 716, 793, 799, 800, 811, 1024, 1124. [Comments on Forster.]

10 LEAVIS, F. R. "E. M. Forster." *The Common Pursuit.* London: Chatto and Windus, 1952, pp. 261-77. Repr. in 41.15.

11 LUCAS, John. "Wagner and Forster: *Parsifal* and *A Room with a View.*" *ELH* 33(1966):92-117.*

12 MC DOWELL, Frederick P. W. "Forster's Many-Faceted Universe: Idea and Paradox in *The Longest Journey.*" *Crit* 4(1961):41-63.*

13 MAC LEAN, Hugh. "The Structure of *A Passage to India.*" *UTQ* 22(1953): 157-71. Repr. in 41.17.

14 MENDILOW, A. A. "The Triadic World of E. M. Forster." See 42.13, pp. 280-91.

15 NIERENBERG, Edwin. "The Prophecy of E. M. Forster." *QQ* 71(1964): 189-202.

16 NIERENBERG, Edwin. "The Withered Priestess: Mrs. Moore's Incomplete Passage to India." *MLQ* 25(1964):198-204. Repr. in 41.17.

17 PRITCHETT, V. S. "Mr. Forster's Birthday." See 16.11, pp. 244-50.

18 RANSOM, John Crowe. "E. M. Forster." *KR* 5(1943):618-23.

19 RICHARDS, I. A. "A Passage to Forster: Reflections on a Novelist." *The Forum* 78(1927):914-20. Repr. in 41.15.

20 SPENDER, Stephen. "Personal Relations and Public Powers." See 9.2, pp. 77-91.

21 WAGGONER, H. H. "Exercises in Perspective: Notes on the Uses of Coincidence in the Novels of E. M. Forster." *Chimera* 3(1945):3-14. Repr. in 41.15.

1 WARREN, Austin. "E. M. Forster." *Rage for Order; Essays in Criticism.* Ann Arbor: U of Michigan P, 1959, pp. 119-41. Repr. in 41.15.*†

2 WHITE, Gertrude. "*A Passage to India*, Analysis and Revaluation." *PMLA* 68(1953):641-57. Repr. in 41.17.*

3 WILSON, Angus. "A Conversation with E. M. Forster." *Encounter* 9(November 1957):52-7.

4 WOOLF, Virginia. "The Novels of E. M. Forster." See 114.15, I, pp. 342-51.

5 WOOLF, Virginia. "The Art of Fiction." See 114.15, II, pp. 51-5.

6 ZABEL, Morton Dauwen. "E. M. Forster: The Trophies of the Mind." See 16.19, pp. 228-52.*

John Galsworthy (1867-1933)

TEXTS

7 *The Works of John Galsworthy.* 30 vols. Manaton Edition. New York: Scribner's, 1922-1936.

8 *The Works of John Galsworthy.* Manaton Edition. 21 vols., with 16 prefaces written by Galsworthy for this ed. London: Heinemann, 1923-1924.

9 *The Forsyte Saga.* Introduction by Percy Hutchinson. New York: Scribner's, 1933. [Modern Standard Authors Series.] †

10 *The Man of Property.* Introduction by Lionel Stevenson. New York: Scribner's, 1922, 1949, 1960. [Modern Standard Authors Series.] †

11 *The Galsworthy Reader.* Ed. and with introduction by Anthony West. New York: Scribner's, 1967. [Contains *The Man of Property*, some plays, and selections from other works.]

12 GARNETT, Edward, ed. *Letters from John Galsworthy, 1900-1932.* Introduction by Garnett. London: Cape; New York: Scribner's, 1934.

BIBLIOGRAPHIES

13 GERBER, Helmut, ed. "John Galsworthy: An Annotated Checklist of Writings About Him." *ELT* 1,iii(1958):7-29.*

14 MARROT, H. *A Bibliography of the Works of John Galsworthy.* London: Mathews and Marrot, 1928.*

15 STEVENS, Earl Eugene. "John Galsworthy: An Annotated Bibliography of Writings About Him. Supplement I." *ELT* 7,ii(1964):93-110.*

CRITICAL AND BIOGRAPHICAL BOOKS

16 BARKER, Dudley. *The Man of Principle: A View of John Galsworthy.* London: Heinemann, 1963.* †

1 KAYE-SMITH, Sheila. *John Galsworthy.* London: Hutchinson, 1916.

2 MARROT, H. *The Life and Letters of John Galsworthy.* New York: Scribner's, 1936. [Standard biography.] *

3 MOTTRAM, Ralph H. *For Some We Loved; An Intimate Portrait of Ada and John Galsworthy.* London: Hutchinson, 1956.*

4 SAUTER, Rudolf. *Galsworthy the Man: An Intimate Portrait.* London: Owen, 1967. [Appendices contain notes by Galsworthy on his works.] *

5 SCHALIT, Leon. *John Galsworthy, a Survey.* New York: Scribner's, 1929.*

6 TAKAHASHI, Genji. *Studies in the Works of John Galsworthy, with Special Reference to His Visions of Love and Beauty.* Tokyo: Shinozaki Shorin, 1954; rev. ed., 1956.

CRITICAL ESSAYS

7 AUSTIN, H. P. "John Galsworthy." *Dublin Review* 189(1931):95-106.

8 BEACH, Joseph Warren. "Variations: Galsworthy." See 11.1, pp. 246-62.*

9 CAZAMIAN, Madeleine. "La pensée de John Galsworthy." *Revue du mois* 15(1913):449-67.*

10 CHEVRILLON, André. *Three Studies in English Literature, Kipling, Galsworthy, Shakespeare.* Port Washington, N.Y.: Kennikat, 1967, pp. 153-219.*

11 COLENUTT, R. "The World of Mr. Galsworthy's Fiction." *Cornhill Magazine* 149(January 1934):55-64.

12 CONRAD, Joseph. "John Galsworthy, An Appreciation." *Tales of Hearsay and Last Essays.* London: Dent, 1955, pp. 125-31.

13 CROFT-COOKE, Rupert. "Grove Lodge." *Cornhill Magazine* 173(Autumn 1962):50-9.

14 CROSS, Wilbur L. "John Galsworthy." *Four Contemporary Novelists.* New York: Macmillan, 1930, pp. 101-53.

15 EAKER, J. Gordon. "Galsworthy and the Modern Mind." *PQ* 29(1950): 31-48.

16 ERVINE, St. John G. *Some Impressions of My Elders.* New York: Macmillan, 1922, pp. 113-60.

17 FAURE, Françoise. "John Galsworthy et les littératures étrangères." *RLC* 22(1948):84-102.

18 FORD, Ford Madox. "John Galsworthy." See 37.17, pp. 165-89.

19 FREEMAN, James C. "Whyte-Melville and Galsworthy's 'Bright Beings.'" *NCF* 5(1950-1951):85-100.

20 FUNKE, Otto. "Zur 'Erlebten Rede' bei Galsworthy." *Englische Studien* 64(1929):450-74. [Indirect monologue.]

1 "Galsworthy and Proust." *TLS* 8(December 1950):777-8.*

2 GROVE, Frederick P. "Morality in *The Forsyte Saga.*" *UTQ* 15(1945-1946): 54-64.*

3 HAMILTON, Robert. "*The Forsyte Saga.*" *QR* 304(1966):431-41.*

4 HARKNESS, Bruce. "Conrad on Galsworthy: The Time Scheme of *Fraternity.*" *MFS* 1(1955):12-3.

5 KETTLE, Arnold. "John Galsworthy: The Man of Property." See 16.7, II, pp. 95-100.

6 LAWRENCE, D. H. "John Galsworthy." *Scrutinies.* Comp. by Edgell Rickword. London: Wishart, 1928, pp. 52-72.*

7 LAWRENCE, D. H. "John Galsworthy." See 72.7, pp. 539-50.

8 LION, Leon M. *The Surprise of My Life: The Lesser Half of an Autobiography.* London: Hutchinson, n.d., pp. 97-100, 119-31, and *passim.* [Contains letters from Galsworthy to actor-manager in his plays.]

9 MAC CARTHY, Desmond. "Galsworthy." *Memories.* New York: Oxford U P, 1953, pp. 55-60.

10 MC CULLOUGH, Bruce. "The Novelist as Social Critic." *Representative English Novelists.* New York: Harper, 1946, pp. 320-35.

11 MUIR, Edwin. See 10.8, pp. 116-24 *passim.*

12 PALLETTE, Drew B. "Young Galsworthy, the Forging of a Satirist." *MP* 56, iii(1959):178-86.

13 PRITCHETT, V. S. "The Forsytes." See 16.11, pp. 282-8.

14 ROSS, Woodburn O. "John Galsworthy: Aspects of an Attitude." *Studies in Honor of John Wilcox.* Ed. A. Dayle Wallace and Woodburn O. Ross. Detroit: Wayne State U P, 1958, pp. 195-208.

15 THIENOVA, Ingeborg. "Der Kritische Realismus bei John Galsworthy." *ZAA* 3(1955):432-46.

16 TILBY, A. Wyatt. "The Epic of Property." *Edinburgh Review* 241(1925): 271-85.*

17 WAGENKNECHT, Edward. "Pity, Irony, and John Galsworthy." See 7.9, pp. 477-93.

David Garnett (1892-)

TEXTS

18 *Lady into Fox* and *A Man at the Zoo.* London: Chatto and Windus, 1960.

19 *Lady into Fox.* With author's note to the present edition and an introduction by Vincent Starrett. New York: Norton, 1966.

1 *The Golden Echo. The Flowers of the Forest. The Familiar Faces.* London: Chatto and Windus, 1953; 1955; 1962. [These three volumes comprise Garnett's autobiography, *The Golden Echo.*]

2 *The White/Garnett Letters.* Ed. Garnett. London: Cape, 1965. [Letters from 1936-1964 by Garnett to a novelist friend.]

3 "Books in General." *New Statesman and Nation* from March 18, 1933 to October 7, 1939. [In these weekly pages Garnett expressed himself as literary critic.]

BIBLIOGRAPHIES

4 *The Garnetts: A Literary Family. An Exhibition.* Austin: U of Texas Humanities Research Center, 1959. [Limited bibliography.]

CRITICAL ESSAYS

5 ELIOT, T. S. "Le roman anglais contemporain (D. H. Lawrence, V. Woolf, D. Garnett, A. Huxley)." *NRF* 28(1927):669-75.

6 HEILBRUN, Caroline G. "Epilogue: David Garnett." *The Garnett Family: The History of a Literary Family.* New York: Macmillan, 1961, pp. 196-201. [See also Bibliography of David Garnett works, Appendix, pp. 209-10.] *

7 HOLROYD, Michael. See 5.1, II, pp. 515-31 and *passim.*

8 IRWIN, W. R. "The Metamorphoses of David Garnett." *PMLA* 73(1958): 386-92.*

George Gissing (1857-1903)

TEXTS
There is no collected edition.

9 *Workers in the Dawn.* Introduction by Robert Shafer. 2 vols. Garden City, N.Y.: Doubleday, Doran, 1935.

10 *The Private Papers of Henry Ryecroft.* Introduction by V. S. Pritchett. New York: Signet Classics, 1961.†

11 *New Grub Street.* Ed. and with introduction by Irving Howe. Boston: Houghton Mifflin, 1962.†

12 *New Grub Street.* Introduction by John Gross. London: Bodley Head, 1967.

13 *New Grub Street.* Introduction by G. W. Stonier. London: Oxford U P, 1958.†

14 *A Life's Morning.* Introduction by William Plomer. 3 vols. London: Home and Van Thal, 1947.

15 *The Odd Women.* 3 vols. London: Doughty Library Series, 1968.

16 *Born in Exile.* Introduction by Walter Allen. London: Gollancz, 1970.

1 *In the Year of Jubilee.* 3 vols. Introduction by William Plomer. London: Watergate Classics, 1947.

2 *The House of Cobwebs and Other Stories.* Introduction by Thomas Seccombe. London: Constable, 1906. [Frequently repr.]

3 *Charles Dickens: A Critical Study.* Port Washington, N.Y.: Kennikat, 1966.*

4 *Selections Autobiographical and Imaginative from the Works of George Gissing.* Biographical and critical notes by his son. Introduction by Virginia Woolf. London: Cape, 1929.

5 GISSING, Algernon and Ellen, eds. *Letters of George Gissing to Members of His Family.* London: Constable, 1927.

6 GETTMANN, Royal, ed. *George Gissing and H. G. Wells, Their Friendship and Correspondence.* Urbana, Ill.: U of Illinois P, 1961.*

7 YOUNG, Arthur C., ed. *The Letters of George Gissing to Eduard Bertz, 1887-1903.* New Brunswick: Rutgers U P, 1961.*

8 COUSTILLAS, Pierre, ed. *The Letters of George Gissing to Gabrielle Fleury.* New York: New York Pub. Lib., 1965.*

9 KORG, Jacob, ed. *George Gissing's Commonplace Book.* New York: New York Pub. Lib., 1962.

BIBLIOGRAPHIES

10 DONNELLY, Mabel Collins, "Bibliography." See 48.15, pp. 225-9.*

11 GERBER, Helmut, ed. *ELT.* The following numbers have annotated bibliographies of writings about Gissing: 1,i(1957):24-8. 1,ii(1958):31-2. 1,iii(1958):36. 2,i(1959):45-6. 3,i(1960):27-30. 3,ii(1960):3-33. 7,i(1964): 14-26. 7,ii(1964):73-92. 8,v(1965):290-300.*

12 GORDAN, John D. *George Gissing: 1857-1903.* New York: New York Pub. Lib., 1954. [Catalogue for an exhibition of materials from the Berg Collection of the New York Public Library.]

13 KORG, Jacob. "Selected Bibliography." See 49.1, pp. 301-5.

14 KORG, Jacob. "George Gissing." *Victorian Fiction: A Guide to Research.* Ed. Lionel Stevenson. Cambridge, Mass.: Harvard U P, 1964, pp. 401-13. [Gives summary of critical work on Gissing up to 1961.] *

CRITICAL AND BIOGRAPHICAL BOOKS

15 DONNELLY, Mabel Collins. *George Gissing: Grave Comedian.* Cambridge, Mass.: Harvard U P, 1954.*

16 GAPP, Samuel Vogt. *George Gissing, Classicist.* Philadelphia: U of Pennsylvania P, 1936.

1 KORG, Jacob. *George Gissing: A Critical Biography.* Seattle: U of Washington P, 1963.*

2 ROBERTS, Morley. *The Private Life of Henry Maitland.* Ed. and with introduction by Morchard Bishop. London: Richards, 1958. [Fictionalized biography.] *

3 SWINNERTON, Frank. *George Gissing: A Critical Study.* 3d ed. Port Washington, N.Y.: Kennikat, 1966.

4 WARD, A. C. *Gissing.* London: Longmans, Green, 1959. [British Council Pamphlet. Selected bibliography, pp. 38-43.]

CRITICAL ESSAYS
The first title is a collection.

5 COUSTILLAS, Pierre, ed. *Collected Articles on George Gissing.* London: Cass, 1968.*

6 ADAMS, Ruth. "George Gissing and Clara Collet." *NCF* 11(1956):72-7.

7 BERGONZI, Bernard. "The Novelist as Hero." *TC* 164(1958):444-55.

8 CAZAMIAN, Madeleine. See 4.9, I, pp. 302-71.*

9 COPE, J. I. "Definition as Structure in *The Ryecroft Papers.*" *MFS* 3(Summer 1957):127-40. Repr. in 49.5.

10 COUSTILLAS, Pierre. "Gissing's Feminine Portraiture." *ELT* 6,iii(1963): 130-41.

11 DALEY, N. L. "Some Reflections on the Scholarship of Gissing." *CJ* 38(1942):21-30.

12 FRIERSON, William C. *L'influence du naturalisme français sur les romanciers anglais de 1885 à 1900.* Paris: Giard, 1925, pp. 205-18.

13 GETTMANN, Royal. "Bentley and Gissing." *NCF* 11(1957):306-14.

14 GISSING, Ellen. "George Gissing: A Character Sketch." *Nineteenth Century and After* 102(1927):417-24. [By Gissing's sister.]

15 GISSING, Ellen. "Some Personal Recollections of George Gissing." *Blackwood's Magazine* 225(1929):653-60.

16 "Gissing's Heroines." *TLS* (28 December 1956):780. Repr. in Coustillas, 49.5.

17 HICKS, Granville. *Figures of Transition: A Study of British Literature at the End of the Nineteenth Century.* New York: Macmillan, 1939, pp. 178-203.

18 HOWE, Irving. "George Gissing: Poet of Fatigue." *A World More Attractive: A View of Modern Literature and Politics.* New York: Horizon, 1963, pp. 109-91. Repr. in 49.5.*

19 KIRK, Russell. "Who Knows George Gissing?" *WHR* 4(1950):213-22. Repr. in 49.5.

1 LEAVIS, Q. D. "Gissing and the English Novel." *Scrutiny* 7(1938):73-81.

2 MORE, Paul Elmer. "George Gissing." *Shelburne Essays.* 5th Ser. New York: Putnam, 1908, pp. 45-65.

3 ORWELL, George. "George Gissing." *LonM* 7(June 1960):36-43. Repr. in 49.5*

4 "The Permanent Stranger." *TLS* (14 February 1948):92. Repr. in 49.5.

5 PRITCHETT, V. S. "Books in General." *New Statesman and Nation* 34(November 8, 1947):372.

6 PRITCHETT, V. S. " 'Grub Street.' " See 16.11, pp. 154-60. Repr. in 49.5.

7 ROBERTS, Morley. "The Letters of George Gissing." *VQR* 7(1931):409-26.

8 SHAFER, Robert. "The Vitality of George Gissing." *American Review* 5(1935):459-87.

9 THOMAS, J. D. "The Public Purposes of George Gissing." *NCF* 8(1953): 118-23.

10 WELLS, H. G. See 109.9, pp. 481-94.

11 WELLS, H. G. "The Novels of Mr. George Gissing." *Contemporary Review* 72(August 1897):192-201.*

12 WELLS, H. G. "George Gissing, An Impression." *Monthly Review* 16(1904): 160-72.*

13 WILLIAMS, Raymond. *Culture and Society, 1780-1950.* New York: Columbia U P, 1958, pp. 172-9.*†

14 WOLFF, Joseph J. "Gissing's Revision of *The Unclassed.*" *NCF* 8(1953): 42-52.

15 WOOLF, Virginia. "George Gissing." See 114.15, I, pp. 297-301.

16 YOUNG, Arthur C. "The Death of Gissing: A Fourth Report." *Essays in Literary History.* Ed. Rudolph Kirk and C. F. Main. New Brunswick: Rutgers U P, 1960, pp. 217-28.

17 YOUNG, Arthur C. "Gissing and Bertz." See 48.7, pp. xix-xl.*

William Golding (1911-)

TEXTS

18 *Lord of the Flies.* Casebook ed.: Text, Criticism, and Notes. Ed. James R. Baker and Arthur P. Ziegler, Jr. New York: Putnam, 1964, 1969. [Includes critical articles on this novel.] * †

19 *Lord of the Flies.* With introduction by E. M. Forster. New York: Coward-McCann, 1962.

1 *Lord of the Flies.* School ed. with introduction and notes by Ian Gregor and Mark Kinkead-Weekes. London: Faber and Faber, 1962. [Editors' notes include definitions of English schoolboy slang.]

2 *The Inheritors.* Educational ed. with introduction and notes by Ian Gregor and Mark Kinkead-Weekes. London: Faber and Faber, 1964.

3 *The Hot Gates and Other Occasional Pieces.* London: Faber and Faber, 1965; New York: Harcourt, Brace and World, 1966. [Among contents see esp. "Fable," Golding's lecture relating to *Lord of the Flies.*] †

BIBLIOGRAPHIES

For selected bibliography see CRITICAL BOOKS below.

CRITICAL AND BIOGRAPHICAL BOOKS

4 BABB, Howard S. *The Novels of William Golding.* Columbus, Ohio: Ohio State U P, 1970.

5 BAKER, James R. *William Golding: A Critical Study.* New York: St. Martin's, 1965. [Contains bibliography.] *

6 DICK, Bernard F. *William Golding.* New York: Twayne, 1967. [Contains annotated bibliography.]

7 HYNES, Samuel. *William Golding.* New York and London: Columbia U P, 1964. [Columbia Essays on Modern Writers. Contains bibliography.]

8 KINKEAD-WEEKES, Mark, and Ian GREGOR. *William Golding: A Critical Study.* London: Faber and Faber, 1967; New York: Harcourt, 1968.*

9 OLDSEY, Bernard S., and Stanley WEINTRAUB. *The Art of William Golding.* New York: Harcourt, Brace and World, 1965. Bloomington: Indiana U P, 1968. [Includes bibliography of Golding's books and essays.]

CRITICAL ESSAYS

The first two titles are collections.

10 NELSON, William, ed. *William Golding's* Lord of the Flies. *A Source Book.* New York: Odyssey, 1963. [Collection contains 17 critical essays.] *†

11 "A William Golding Miscellany." *Studies in the Literary Imagination* 2,ii. Atlanta: Georgia State Col., 1969. [6 articles on *Pincher Martin, The Spire,* and *The Pyramid.*]

12 BABB, Howard S. "Four Passages from William Golding's Fiction." *MinnR* 5(1965):50-8.

13 BUFKIN, E. C. "*Lord of the Flies*: An Analysis." *GaR* 19(1965):40-57.

14 BUFKIN, E. C. "The Ironic Art of William Golding's *The Inheritors.*" *TSLL* 9(1968):567-78.

15 CIXOUS-BERGER, Hélène. "L'allégorie du mal dans l'oeuvre de William Golding." *Critique* (Paris) 22, no. 227(1966):309-20.

1 CRAMPTON, D. W. "*The Spire.*" *CritQ* 9(1967):63-79.

2 DIERICKX, J. "Le thème de la chute dans les romans de W. Golding." *EA* 16(1963):230-42.

3 HENRY, Avril. "William Golding: *The Pyramid.*" *Southern Review* (U of Adelaide) 3,i(1968):5-31.

4 KERMODE, Frank. "The Novels of William Golding." *International Literary Annual*, no. 3. Ed. John Wain. London: Calder, 1961, pp. 11-29. Also in 16.6, pp. 198-213. Also in 51.10.*

5 KERMODE, Frank, and William GOLDING. "The Meaning of It All." *Books and Bookmen* 5(1959):9-10. [BBC discussion.]

6 PETER, John. "The Fables of William Golding." *KR* 19(1957):577-92. Also in 51.10.*

7 QUINN, M. "An Unheroic Hero: William Golding's 'Pincher Martin.' " *CritQ* 4(1962):247-56.

8 ROPER, Derek. "Allegory and Novel in Golding's *The Spire.*" *WSCL* 8(1967):19-30.

9 TALON, Henri. "Irony in *Lord of the Flies.*" *EIC* 18(1968):296-309.*

Henry Green (pseud. Henry Vincent Yorke) (1905-)

TEXTS

10 *Pack My Bag.* London: Hogarth, 1940. [Autobiographical.]

11 "A Novelist to His Readers." *Listener* 44(November 9, 1950):505-6; 45 (March 15, 1951):425-7.

12 "A Fire, a Flood, and the Price of Meat." *Listener* 46(August 23, 1951): 293-4.

13 "A propos du roman non representatif." *Roman* 3(June 1951):238-45.

14 "An Unfinished Novel." *LonM* 6(April 1959):11-7.

BIBLIOGRAPHY

15 WEATHERHEAD, A. K. "Bibliography." See 53.1, pp. 169-70. [Selected bibliography.]

CRITICAL AND BIOGRAPHICAL BOOKS

16 RUSSELL, John David. *Henry Green: Nine Novels and an Unpacked Bag.* New Brunswick: Rutgers U P, 1960.

17 STOKES, Edward. *The Novels of Henry Green.* London: Hogarth, 1959.*

1 WEATHERHEAD, A. K. *A Reading of Henry Green.* Seattle: U of Washington P, 1961.

CRITICAL ESSAYS

2 ALLEN, Walter. "An Artist of the Thirties." *Folios of New Writing* 3(Spring 1941):149-58.

3 ALLEN, Walter. "Henry Green." *Penguin New Writing* 25(1945):144-55. Repr. in *Modern British Writing.* Ed. Denys Val Baker. New York: Vanguard, 1947, pp. 258-71.*

4 CHURCHILL, Thomas. "*Loving:* A Comic Novel." *Crit* 4(1961):29-38.

5 DAVIDSON, Barbara. "The World of *Loving.*" *WSCL* 2(1961):65-78.*

6 GILL, Brendan. "Something." *NY* 26(March 25, 1950):111-2.

7 HALL, James. "Paradoxes of Pleasure-and-Pain: Henry Green." See 16.2, pp. 66-81.

8 HOWARD, Jean. "Selected Notice." *Horizon* 18(1948):365-6. [Review of *Concluding.*]

9 HOWE, Irving. "Fiction Chronicle." *PR* 16(1949):1052-5. [Review of *Loving.*]

10 JOHNSON, Bruce. "Henry Green's Comic Symbolism." *BSUF* 6,iii(1965): 29-35.

11 KARL, Frederick. "Normality Defined: The Novels of Henry Green." See 16.5, pp. 183-200.

12 KETTLE, Arnold. "Henry Green: *Party Going.*" See 16.7, II, pp. 190-7.

13 LABOR, Earle. "Henry Green's Web of Loving." *Crit* 4(1961):29-40.

14 LEHMANN, Rosamond. "An Absolute Gift." *TLS* (August 6,1954):xli. [Review of *Loving.*]

15 MELCHIORI, Giorgio. "The Abstract Art of Henry Green." See 14.17, pp. 188-212.*

16 PHELPS, Robert. "The Vision of Henry Green." *HudR* 5(1953):614-20.*

17 PRITCHETT, V. S. "Green on Doting." *NY* 28(May 17, 1952):137-42.

18 QUINTON, A. "A French View of *Loving.*" *LonM* 6(April 1959):25-35.

19 ROSS, Alan. "Green, with Envy: Critical Reflections and an Interview." *LonM* 6(April 1959):18-24.

20 RUSSELL, John. "There It Is." *KR* 26(1964):433-65. [Based on interview with Green.] *

21 SHAPIRO, Stephen A. "Henry Green's *Back*: The Presence of the Past." *Crit* 7(1964):87-96.

22 SOUTHERN, Terry. "Henry Green et l'art du roman." *LetN* 13(March-April 1965):116-33. [Interview.]

1 TAYLOR, Donald S. "Catalytic Rhetoric: Henry Green's Theory of the Modern Novel." *Criticism* 7(1965):81-99.*

2 TINDALL, William York. See 12.22, pp. 92-7.

3 TOYNBEE, Philip. "The Novels of Henry Green." *PR* 16(1949):487-97.*

4 TURNER, Myron. "The Imagery of Wallace Stevens and Henry Green." *WSCL* 8(1967):60-77.

5 WELTY, Eudora. "Henry Green, a Novelist of the Imagination." *TQ* 4(1961):246-56.*

Graham Greene (1904-)

TEXTS

6 *Graham Greene's Works.* Uniform Edition. London: Heinemann, 1947- . [The Uniform Edition is not complete. Some novels contain alterations from the first editions.]

7 *The Power and the Glory.* Introduction by Greene. New York: Viking, 1958. [In addition to this, there are numerous paperbacks of Greene's novels.] †

8 *Collected Essays.* London: Bodley Head; New York: Viking, 1969. [Includes many but not all of the essays in *The Lost Childhood and Other Essays.* London: Eyre and Spottiswoode, 1952.]

9 *Why Do I Write? An Exchange of Views Between Elizabeth Bowen, Graham Greene and V. S. Pritchett.* London: Marshall, 1948.

BIBLIOGRAPHIES

A comprehensive bibliography is in preparation.

10 BEEBE, Maurice. "Criticism of Graham Greene: A Selected Checklist with an Index to Studies of Separate Works." *MFS* 3,iii(1957):281-8.*

11 BIRMINGHAM, William. "Graham Greene Criticism." *Thought* 27(Spring 1952):71-100.*

12 BRENNAN, Neil. "Bibliography." See 55.13, Evans, pp. 245-76.

13 HARGREAVES, Phyllis. "Graham Greene: A Selected Bibliography." *MFS* 3,iii(1957):269-80.*

CRITICAL AND BIOGRAPHICAL BOOKS

14 ALLOTT, Kenneth, and Miriam FARRIS. *The Art of Graham Greene.* London: Hamilton, 1951.*

1 DE PANGE, Victor. *Graham Greene.* Paris: Editions Universitaires, 1953.*

2 DE VITIS, A. A. *Graham Greene.* New York: Twayne, 1964. [Contains annotated bibliography.]

3 KUNKEL, Francis L. *The Labyrinthine Ways of Graham Greene.* New York: Sheed and Ward, 1960.

4 LODGE, David. *Graham Greene.* New York: Columbia U P, 1966. [Columbia Essays on Modern Writers.]

5 MADAULE, Jacques. *Graham Greene.* Paris: Editions du Temps Présent, 1949.*

6 MATHEWS, Ronald. *Mon Ami, Graham Greene.* Paris: Desclée de Brouwer, 1957. [Biographical.]

7 MESNET, Marie-Béatrice. *Graham Greene and* The Heart of the Matter. London: Cresset, 1954.

8 PRYCE-JONES, David. *Graham Greene.* Edinburgh: Oliver and Boyd, 1963.

9 RISCHIK, Josef. *Graham Greene und Sein Werk.* Bern: Francke, 1951.

10 ROSTENNE, Paul. *Graham Greene témoin des temps tragiques.* Paris: Julliard, 1949.*

11 STRATFORD, Philip. *Faith and Fiction: Creative Process in Greene and Mauriac.* Notre Dame: U of Notre Dame P, 1964.†

12 WYNDHAM, Francis. *Graham Greene.* London: Longmans, Greene, 1955. [British Council pamphlet. Selected bibliography.]

CRITICAL ESSAYS

The first three titles are collections.

13 EVANS, Robert O., ed. *Graham Greene: Some Critical Considerations.* Lexington, Ky.: U of Kentucky P, 1963.*

14 *MFS* 3, iii(1957). Graham Greene Special Number.

15 *Ren* 12(Fall 1959). Graham Greene Special Number.

16 ALBERES, René. "Graham Greene et responsibilités." *Les hommes traqués.* Paris: La Nouvelle Editions, 1953, pp. 157-85.

17 ALLEN, Walter. "The Novels of Graham Greene." *Penguin New Writing* 18(1943):148-60.*

18 BARRATT, Harold. "Adultery as Betrayal in Graham Greene." *DR* 45(1965):324-32.

19 BOARDMAN, Gwenn R. "Greene's *Under the Garden:* Aesthetic Explorations." *Ren* 17(1965):180-90, 194.

20 CALDER-MARSHALL, Arthur. "The Works of Graham Greene." *Horizon* 1(1940):367-75.

21 DOOLEY, D. J. "The Suspension of Disbelief: Greene's *Burnt-Out Case.*" *DR* 43(1963):343-52.

1 DUFFY, Joseph. "The Lost World of Graham Greene." *Thought* 33(1958): 229-47.

2 ELLIS, William D., Jr. "The Grand Theme of Graham Greene." *SWR* 41(1956):239-50.

3 GREGOR, Ian, and Brian NICHOLAS. "Grace and Morality: *Thérèse Desqueroux; The End of the Affair.*" See 14.3, pp. 185-216.

4 GROB, Alan. *The Power and the Glory*, Graham Greene's Argument from Design." *Criticism* 11,i(1969):1-30.

5 GRUBBS, Henry A. "Albert Camus and Graham Greene." *MLQ* 10(March 1949):33-42.

6 HOGGART, Richard. "The Force of Caricature: Aspects of the Art of Graham Greene with Particular Reference to *The Power and the Glory.*" *EIC* 3(1953):447-62.*

7 HORTMANN, Wilhelm. "Graham Greene: The Burnt-Out Catholic." *TCL* 10(1964):64-76.

8 IVASCHOVA, V. "Legende und Wahrheit über Graham Greene." *ZAA* 10(1962):229-58.

9 KERMODE, Frank. "Mr. Greene's Eggs and Crosses." See 16.6, pp. 176-87.*

10 KERMODE, Frank. "The House of Fiction: Interviews with Seven English Novelists." *PR* 30(Spring 1963):61-82. [Includes Greene.]

11 KETTLE, Arnold. "Graham Greene: *The Heart of the Matter.*" See 16.7, II, pp. 170-7.

12 LERNER, Lawrence. "Graham Greene." *CritQ* 5(1963):217-31.

13 LEWIS, R. W. B. "Graham Greene: The Religious Affair." See 14.13, pp. 220-74.*

14 MARIAN, Sister I. H. M. "Graham Greene's People: Being and Becoming." *Ren* 18(1965):16-22.

15 MC CALL, Dan. "*Brighton Rock*: The Price of Order." *English Language Notes* 3(1966):290-4.

16 MARTIN, Graham. "Novelists of Three Decades: Evelyn Waugh, Graham Greene, C. P. Snow." See 8.3, Ford, pp. 401-9.

17 MUELLER, William R. "The Theme of Love: Graham Greene's *The Heart of the Matter.*" See 14.19, pp. 136-57.

18 NEIS, Edgar. "Zum Sprachstil Graham Greenes." *NS* 6(1957):166-73.*

19 NOXON, James. "Kierkegaard's Stages and *A Burnt-Out Case.*" *REL* 3(1962):90-101.

20 O'DONNELL, D. "Graham Greene: The Anatomy of Pity." See 15.2, pp. 63-94.

21 O'FAOLAIN, Sean. "Graham Greene: I Suffer, Therefore I Am." See 15.3, pp. 73-97.

1 ORWELL, George. "Review of *The Heart of the Matter.*" *NY* 24(July 17, 1948):66. Repr. in 92.11, IV, pp. 439-43.

2 SACKVILLE-WEST, Edward. "The Electric Hare: Some Aspects of Graham Greene." *Month* 6(September 1951):141-7.

3 SEWARD, Barbara. "Graham Greene, a Hint of an Explanation." *Western Review* 22(1958):83-95.

4 SEWELL, Elizabeth. "Graham Greene." *Dublin Review* 228(1954):12-21.

5 SHUTTLEWORTH, Martin, and Simon RAVEN. "The Art of Fiction III: Graham Greene." *ParR* 1(Autumn 1953):24-41. [Interview.]

6 TRAVERSI, Derek. "Graham Greene: The Earlier Novels"; "Graham Greene: The Later Novels." *TC* 149(1951):231-40; 318-28.

7 TURNELL, Martin. "Graham Greene: The Man Within." *Ramparts* 4(June 1965):53-64.

8 VOORHEES, Richard. "Recent Greene." *SAQ* 62(Spring 1963):244-55.

9 WAUGH, Evelyn. "Felix Culpa?" *Cweal* 48(July 16, 1948):322-5. [Review of *The Power and the Glory.*]

10 WEST, Paul. "Graham Greene." *The Wine of Absurdity: Essays on Literature and Consolation.* University Park, Pa.: Pennsylvania State U P, 1966, pp. 174-85.

11 WICHERT, Robert A. "The Quality of Graham Greene's Mercy." *CE* 25(1963):99-103.

12 WILSHERE, A. D. "Conflict and Conciliation in Graham Greene." *E&S* 29(1966):122-37.

13 WOODCOCK, George. "Graham Greene." See 15.15, pp. 125-53.

14 ZABEL, Morton D. "Graham Greene the Best and the Worst." See 16.19, pp. 276-96.*

James Hanley (1901-)

TEXTS

15 *The Works of James Hanley.* Uniform Edition. London: Nicholson and Watson, 1944- .

16 *Men in Darkness: Five Stories.* Preface by John Cowper Powys. London: Lane, 1931. [Uniform Edition, 1948.]

17 *Broken Water: An Autobiographical Excursion.* London: Chatto and Windus, 1937.*

18 "Toccata in C Minor: An Autobiographical Fragment." *London Mercury* 36(June 1937):234-8.

19 "Minority Report." *Fortnightly* 159(June 1943):419-22.

20 "A Writer's Day." In Hanley, *Don Quixote Drowned.* London: Macdonald, 1953, pp. 57-83.

BIBLIOGRAPHIES

There is no separate bibliography.

1 Bibliography of Hanley's works in 58.2, pp. 203-4.

CRITICAL AND BIOGRAPHICAL BOOKS

2 STOKES, Edward. *The Novels of James Hanley.* Melbourne: Cheshire, 1964.*

CRITICAL ESSAYS

3 "The Kingdom of the Sea." *TLS* (February 27, 1953):136.*

4 KUNITZ, Stanley J., and Howard HAYCRAFT. See 3.15, p. 611.

5 LAWRENCE, T. E. *The Letters of T. E. Lawrence.* Ed. David Garnett. Garden City, N.Y.: Doubleday, Doran, 1939, pp. 727-9, 730-1, 734-6, 737-8, 847-8, 864. [Letters from Lawrence to Hanley about the latter's writing.]

6 MOORE, Reginald. "The Sea Around Him." *John O'London's Weekly* (September 19, 1952).*

7 "The New Novels: Continuing The Furys." *TLS*(July 18, 1936):597. [Review of *The Secret Journey.*]

8 POWYS, John Cowper. "Preface." See 57.16, pp. xi-xiv.

9 PRITCHETT, V. S. "Fiction." *Spectator* 157(August 7, 1936):250.

L. (Leslie) P. (Poles) Hartley (1895-)

TEXTS

10 *Eustace and Hilda: A Trilogy.* Introduction by Lord David Cecil. London: Putnam; New York: British Book Centre, 1958. [The three novels with the addition of *Hilda's Letter* published separately in Faber Paper Covered Editions. London: Faber and Faber, 1964-1965.]†

11 *The Go-Between.* London: Hamilton, 1953.†

12 *The Collected Short Stories.* London: Hamilton, 1968.

13 *The Novelist's Responsibility.* London: Hamilton, 1967. [Essays.] *

BIBLIOGRAPHIES

14 BIEN, Peter. "Bibliography." See 59.1, pp. 267-9. [A more complete version of this in 59.2.]

CRITICAL AND BIOGRAPHICAL BOOKS

1 BIEN, Peter. *L. P. Hartley*. London: Chatto and Windus, 1963.

CRITICAL ESSAYS
The first title is a collection.

2 *Adam International Review* 29, nos. 294-5-6(1961). L. P. Hartley Number.

3 ATHOS, John. "L. P. Hartley and the Gothic Infatuation." *TCL* 7(1962): 172-9.

4 BLOOMFIELD, Paul. "L. P. Hartley." Paul Bloomfield and Bernard Bergonzi, *Anthony Powell and L. P. Hartley*. London: Longmans, Green, 1962. [British Council pamphlet.]

5 CECIL, Lord David. "Introduction." See 58.10, pp. 7-13.*

6 CLOSS, August. "Leslie Poles Hartley." *NS* 6(1957):39-42.

7 HALL, James. "Games of Apprehension: L. P. Hartley." See 16.2, pp. 111-28.

8 MELCHIORI, Giorgio. "The English Novelist and the American Tradition." *SR* 68(1960):502-15.*

9 VERNIER, J.-P. "La trilogie romanesque de L. P. Hartley." *EA* 13(1960): 26-31.*

10 WEBSTER, Harvey Curtis. "The Novels of L. P. Hartley." *Crit* 4,ii(1961): 39-51.*

Richard Hughes (1900-)

TEXTS

11 *A High Wind in Jamaica or The Innocent Voyage*. Foreword by Vernon Watkins. New York: Signet, 1961.†

12 *Richard Hughes: An Omnibus*. New York: Harper, 1931. [Autobiographical introduction, pp. vii-xxxvi.]

BIBLIOGRAPHIES AND CRITICAL BOOKS
There are no separate bibliographies or critical books.

CRITICAL ESSAYS

13 ALLEN, Walter. See 7.10, pp. 58-62.*

1 HENIGHAN, J. T. "Nature and Convention in *A High Wind in Jamaica.*" *Crit* 9(1966):5-18.

2 ORME, Daniel. "Au coeur d'un cyclone avec M. Richard Hughes." *Le Mois* (October 1938):212-7.

3 WOODWARD, Daniel. "The Delphic Voice: Richard Hughes's *A High Wind in Jamaica.*" *PELL* 3(Winter 1967):57-74.

Aldous Huxley (1894-1963)

TEXTS

A number of the novels are available in paperback, several being in the Harper and Row Perennial Library.

4 *The Works of Aldous Huxley.* Collected Edition. London: Chatto and Windus, 1946- .

5 *Brave New World.* With a foreword by Huxley. Introduction by Charles J. Rolo. New York: Harper, 1960.†

6 *Brave New World and Brave New World Revisited.* Foreword by Huxley. Introduction by Charles J. Rolo. New York: Harper, 1960.†

7 *Brave New World and Brave New World Revisited.* Introduction by Martin Green. Foreword by Huxley. New York: Harper, 1965.†

8 *Brave New World and Brave New World Revisited.* Introduction by C. P. Snow. New York: Harper and Row, 1963.†

9 *Point Counter Point.* Introduction by C. P. Snow. New York: Harper and Row, 1963.†

10 *Antic Hay and The Gioconda Smile.* Introduction by Martin Green. New York: Harper and Row, 1963.†

11 *The Devils of Loudon.* New York: Harper, 1959.†

12 *Selected Essays.* Ed. by Harold Raymond. Introduction by Frank Whitehead. London: Chatto and Windus, 1961. [Queen's Classics.]

13 *The World of Aldous Huxley: An Omnibus of His Fiction and Non-Fiction over Three Decades.* Ed. and with introduction by Charles J. Rolo. New York: Smith, 1968, [Anthology of prose and poetry with *Antic Hay* complete.]

14 *Letters of Aldous Huxley.* Ed. Grover Smith. London: Chatto and Windus, 1969.*

BIBLIOGRAPHIES

15 CLARESON, Thomas D., and Carolyn S. ANDREWS. "Aldous Huxley: A Bibliography 1960-1964." *Extrapolation* 6(1964):2-21. [Supplements Eschelbach and Shober.] *

16 ESCHELBACH, Claire John, and Joyce Lee SHOBER. *Aldous Huxley: A Bibliography 1916-1959.* Berkeley: U of California P, 1961.*

CRITICAL AND BIOGRAPHICAL BOOKS

1 ATKINS, John. *Aldous Huxley: A Literary Study.* New York: Orion, 1967.

2 BOWERING, Peter. *Aldous Huxley: A Study of the Major Novels.* Oxford: Athlone P, 1968.

3 BROOKE, Jocelyn. *Aldous Huxley.* London: Longmans, Green, 1954. [British Council pamphlet.]

4 CLARK, Ronald W. *The Huxleys.* London: Heinemann, 1968. [Biography.]

5 HEINTZ-FRIEDRICH, Suzanne. *Aldous Huxley; Entwicklung seiner Metaphysik.* Bern: Francke, 1949.

6 HENDERSON, Alexander. *Aldous Huxley.* New York: Russell and Russell, 1964.*

7 HOLMES, Charles. *Aldous Huxley and the Way to Reality.* Bloomington: Indiana U P, 1970.

8 HUXLEY, Julian, ed. *Aldous Huxley 1894-1963. A Memorial Volume.* London: Chatto and Windus, 1965.

9 JOUGUELET, Pierre. *Aldous Huxley.* Paris: Editions du Temps Présent, 1948.

10 MECKIER, Jerome. *Aldous Huxley: Satire and Structure.* London: Chatto and Windus, 1969.*

CRITICAL ESSAYS

11 BALDENSPERGER, F. "Les petits illogismes d'un grand romancier: Une hypothèse historique d'Aldous Huxley." *Essays in Honor of Albert Feuillerat.* Ed. Henri M. Peyre. New Haven: Yale U P, 1943, pp. 255-65. [Yale Romantic Studies, 22.] *

12 BARTLETT, Norman. "Aldous Huxley and D. H. Lawrence." *AusQ* 36, i(1964):76-84.*

13 BEACH, Joseph W. "Counterpoint: Aldous Huxley." See 11.1, pp. 458-69.*

14 BIRNBAUM, Milton. "Aldous Huxley's Conception of the Nature of Reality." *Person* 47(1966):297-314.

15 BULLOUGH, Geoffrey. "Aspects of Aldous Huxley." *ES* 30(1949): 233-43.*

16 CHASE, Richard. "The Huxley-Heard Paradise." *PR* 10(1943):143-58.

17 DYSON, A. E. "Aldous Huxley and the Two Nothings." *CritQ* 3(1961): 293-309. Repr. in 11.10, pp. 166-86.*

18 EATON, Gai. "Monk at Large: Aldous Huxley." *The Richest Vein.* London: Faber and Faber, 1949, pp. 166-82.

19 ENROTH, Clyde. "Mysticism in Two of Aldous Huxley's Early Novels." *TCL* 6(1961):123-32.

1 ESTRICH, H. W. "Jesting Pilate Tells the Answer." *SR* 47(1939):63-81.

2 GLICKSBERG, Charles I. "The Intellectual Pilgrimage of Aldous Huxley." *DR* 19(1939):165-78.

3 GRUSHOW, Ira. "*Brave New World* and *The Tempest*." *CE* 24(1962):42-5.

4 HACKER, A. "Dostoevsky's Disciples: Man and Sheep in Political Theory." *Journal of Politics* 17(1955):590-613.

5 HAUSERMANN, Hans W. "Aldous Huxley as a Literary Critic." *PMLA* 48(1933):908-18.*

6 HEARD, Gerald. "The Poignant Prophet." *KR* 27(1965):49-70.

7 HOFFMAN, F. J. "Aldous Huxley and the Novel of Ideas." See 10.9, O'Connor, pp. 189-200.*

8 HUXLEY, Aldous, and John MORGAN. "Aldous Huxley on Contemporary Society." *Listener* 67(1961):237-9.

9 ISHERWOOD, Christopher. "Aldous Huxley in California." *Atlantic Monthly* 214(September 1964):44-7.

10 JOAD, C. E. M. "Aldous Huxley and the Dowagers." *Return to Philosophy*. London: Faber and Faber, 1955, pp. 78-94 and *passim.*

11 KETTLE, Arnold. "Aldous Huxley: *Point Counter Point.*" See 16.7, II, pp. 167-70.

12 KING, Carlyle. "Aldous Huxley and Music." *QQ* 70(1963):336-51.*

13 MAUROIS, André. "Aldous Huxley." *Poets and Prophets.* New York: Harper, 1935, pp. 285-312.

14 MONCH, W. "Der Acte Gratuit und das Schicksalsproblem bei André Gide und Aldous Huxley." *Zeitschrift für Französischen und Englischen Unterricht* 30(1931):429-35.

15 MULLER, H. J. "Apostles of the Lost Generation: Huxley, Hemingway." See 14.20, pp. 383-403.

16 NAZARETH, Peter. "Aldous Huxley and His Critics." *ESA* 7(1964):65-81.*

17 O'FAOLAIN, Sean. "Huxley and Waugh, or, I Do Not Think, Therefore I Am." See 15.3, pp. 33-69.

18 ROBERTS, John H. "Huxley and Lawrence." *VQR* 13(1937):546-57.

19 ROGERS, Winfield H. "Aldous Huxley's Humanism." *SR* 43(1935):262-72.

20 SAVAGE, D. S. "Aldous Huxley and the Dissociation of Personality." *SR* 55(1947):537-68. Repr. in 16.14, pp. 129-55.*

21 SCHMERL, Rudolf B. "The Two Future Worlds of Aldous Huxley." *PMLA* 77(1962):328-34.

22 SPENCER, Theodore. "Aldous Huxley: The Latest Phase." *Atlantic Monthly* 165(1940):407-9.

1 STEWART, D. H. "Aldous Huxley's *Island.*" *QQ* 70(1963):326-35.

2 TEMPLE, R. Z. "Aldous Huxley et la littérature française." *RLC* 19(January-March 1939):65-110.

3 WAUGH, Evelyn, Angus WILSON, Francis WYNDHAM, John WAIN, and Peter QUENNELL. "A Critical Symposium on Aldous Huxley." *LonM* 2(August 1955):51-64.

4 WILSON, Colin. "Existential Criticism and the Work of Aldous Huxley." *LonM* 5(September 1958):46-59.

Christopher Isherwood (1904-)

TEXTS

5 *All the Conspirators: A Novel.* Introduction by Isherwood. London: Cape, 1928; new ed., 1957. New York: Laughlin, 1958.

6 *The Memorial: Portrait of a Family.* London: Hogarth, 1932; Norfolk, Conn.: New Directions, 1946.

7 *The Berlin Stories.* New York: Laughlin, 1945. [*The Last of Mr. Norris* and *Goodbye to Berlin.*]

8 *The Berlin Stories.* New preface by Isherwood. New York: Laughlin, 1954.*

9 *Lions and Shadows: An Education in the Twenties.* London: Hogarth, 1938; Norfolk, Conn.: New Directions, 1947. [Fictionalized autobiography.] *

10 *Exhumations: Stories, Articles, Verses.* London: Methuen; New York: Simon and Schuster, 1966.

11 "Autobiography of an Individual." *TC* 149(1951):405-11. [Review of Spender's *World Within World.* Contains important information on Isherwood.]

12 "Coming to London, 9." See 19.13, pp. 108-17.

13 "Discovering Vedanta." *TC* 170(1961):64-71.

BIBLIOGRAPHIES AND CRITICAL BOOKS

There are no separate bibliographies or critical books.

CRITICAL ESSAYS

14 ALLEN, Walter. See 7.10, pp. 234-8.

15 AMIS, Kingsley. "A Bit Glassy." *The Spectator* 208(March 9, 1962):309. [Review of *Down There on a Visit.*]

16 BANTOCK, G. H. "The Novels of Christopher Isherwood." See 16.12, Rajan, pp. 46-57.*

1 CONNOLLY, Cyril. See 11.8, pp. 82-3; 85-7. [On Isherwood's style.] *

2 DEMPSEY, David. "Connolly, Orwell and Others: An English Miscellany." *AR* 7(1947):142-50.

3 "The Huge Northern Circuit." *TLS* (May 23, 1952):344.*

4 ISHERWOOD, Christopher, and Stanley POSS. "A Conversation on Tape." *LonM* 1(June 1961):41-58.

5 ISHERWOOD, Christopher, and George WICKES. "An Interview with Christopher Isherwood." *Shen* 16(Spring 1956):23-52.

6 JEBB, Julian. "Down There on a Visit." *LonM* 2(April 1962):87-9.

7 KERMODE, Frank. "The Interpretation of the Times (Christopher Isherwood and Anthony Powell)." See 16.6, pp. 121-5.

8 LEHMANN, John. *The Whispering Gallery*, pp. 176, 179-82, 210-3, 232-5, 243-4, 304-8. *I Am My Brother*, pp. 14-5, 31, 64-5, 153-4. *The Ample Proposition*, pp. 28-32, 197-8.

9 MC LAUGHLIN, Richard. "Isherwood's Arrival and Departure." *Saturday Review of Literature* 30(December 27, 1947):14-5.

10 MAES-JELINEK, Hena. "The Knowledge of Man in the Works of Christopher Isherwood." *RLV* 26(1960):341-60.*

11 MAYNE, Richard. "The Novel and Mr. Norris." *Cambridge Journal* 6(1953): 561-70.

12 MITCHELL, Breon. "W. H. Auden and Christopher Isherwood: The 'German Influence.' " *Oxford German Studies* 1(1966):163-72. [On Auden-Isherwood drama.]

13 PRITCHETT, V. S. "Men of the World." *Penguin New Writing* 30(1947): 135-41.

14 PRITCHETT, V. S. "Books in General." *New Statesman and Nation* 44(1952):213-4.*

15 ROSENFELD, Isaac. "Isherwood's Master Theme." *An Age of Enormity; Life and Writing in the Forties and Fifties.* Ed. Theodore Solutaroff. Cleveland: World, 1962, pp. 149-54.

16 SPENDER, Stephen. *World Within World.* New York: Harcourt, Brace, 1951, pp. 91-5, 109-17, 120, 158-9, and *passim.* *

17 TURNER, W. J. "Christopher Isherwood." *Living Writers.* Ed. Gilbert Phelps. London: Sylvan, 1948, pp. 48-57.

18 VIERTEL, Berthold. "Christopher Isherwood and Dr. Friedrich Bergmann." *TArts* 39(May 1946):295-8.

19 WEISGERBER, J. "Les romans et récits de Christopher Isherwood." *Revue de L'Université de Bruxelles* 9-10(July-September 1958):360-79.

20 WILSON, Angus. "The New and the Old Isherwood." *Encounter* 12(August 1954):62-8.

James Joyce (1882-1941)

TEXTS

1 *Dubliners.* Ed. Robert Scholes and Richard Ellmann. New York: Viking, 1967. [Definitive text.] †

2 *A Portrait of the Artist as a Young Man: Text, Criticism, and Notes.* Ed. Chester Anderson. New York: Viking, 1968. [Definitive text prepared by Chester Anderson and Richard Ellmann. Contains also selected criticism and bibliography. Text published in 1964 by Viking.] †

3 *Ulysses.* Hamburg: Odyssey, 1932. 2 vols. [Generally considered the most accurate text.]

4 *Ulysses.* New York: Random House, 1934. [First authorized American edition; frequently repr. Pub. as Modern Library Giant, 1940.]

5 *Finnegans Wake.* New York: Viking, 1939. [First American edition.]

6 *A First-Draft Version of* Finnegans Wake. Ed. and annotated by David Hayman. Austin: U of Texas P, 1963.

7 *Stephen Hero.* Ed. Theodore Spencer. New York: New Directions, 1944, 1955. [First draft of *A Portrait of the Artist as a Young Man.*]

8 *Stephen Hero.* New ed. with added manuscript pages. Ed. John J. Slocum and Herbert Cahoon. Norfolk, Conn.: New Directions, 1963.†

9 *Exiles, a Play in Three Acts.* New York: Viking, 1951. [Includes notes by Joyce and introduction by Padraic Colum.]

10 *Chamber Music.* Ed. with introduction and notes by William York Tindall. New York: Columbia U P, 1954.

11 *The Portable James Joyce.* Ed. H. Levin. New York: Viking, 1947, 1953; rev. ed. 1966. Under title, *The Essential James Joyce.* London: Cape, 1948. [The 1966 edition contains *Dubliners, A Portrait of the Artist, Exiles, Collected Poems,* and selections from *Ulysses* and *Finnegans Wake.*]

12 *Giacomo Joyce.* Introduction and notes by Richard Ellmann. New York: Viking, 1968. [Brief Joyce manuscript, probably finished during summer, 1914.]

13 CONNOLLY, Thomas E., ed. *James Joyce's Scribbledehobble: The Ur-Workbook for* Finnegans Wake. Evanston, Ill.: Northwestern U P, 1961.

14 SCHOLES, Robert, and Richard KAIN, eds. *The Workshop of Daedalus.* Evanston, Ill.: Northwestern U P, 1965. [Important for study of *A Portrait of the Artist.*]

15 *The Critical Writings of James Joyce.* Ed. by Ellsworth Mason and Richard Ellmann. New York: Viking, 1959.†

16 *Letters of James Joyce.* Vol. I ed. by Stuart Gilbert. New York: Viking, 1957. Vols. II and III ed. by Richard Ellmann. New York: Viking, 1966.

BIBLIOGRAPHIES

1 BEEBE, Maurice, and A. Walton LITZ. "Criticism of James Joyce: A Selected Checklist with an Index to Studies of Separate Works." *MFS* 4(Spring 1958):71-99.

2 CONNOLLY, Thomas E. *The Personal Library of James Joyce: A Descriptive Bibliography. U of Buffalo Studies* 20,i(1955). [Monograph.]

3 DEMING, Robert H. *A Bibliography of James Joyce Studies.* Lawrence, Kan.: U of Kansas Libraries, 1964. [Annotated.] *

4 KAIN, Richard M. "Addenda to Deming Bibliography." *James Joyce Quarterly* 3,ii(1966):154-9.*

5 SCHOLES, Robert. *The Cornell Joyce Collection: A Catalogue.* Ithaca, N.Y.: Cornell U P, 1961.

6 SLOCUM, John J., and H. CAHOON. *A Bibliography of James Joyce.* New Haven: Yale U P, 1953.* [Standard bibliography.]

7 SPIELBERG, Peter. *James Joyce's Manuscripts and Letters at the University of Buffalo: A Catalogue.* Buffalo: U of Buffalo, 1962.

8 STALEY, Thomas F. "Joyce Scholarship in the 1960s." *PELL* 1(1965): 279-86.*

WORD INDEXES AND HANDBOOKS

9 CAMPBELL, J., and H. M. ROBINSON. *A Skeleton Key to* Finnegans Wake. New York: Harcourt, Brace, 1944.

10 GLASHEEN, Adaline. *A Second Census of* Finnegans Wake. Evanston, Ill.: Northwestern U P, 1963.

11 HANLEY, Miles L. *Word Index to James Joyce's* Ulysses. Madison: U of Wisconsin P, 1937, 1951.

12 HART, Clive. *A Concordance to* Finnegans Wake. Minneapolis: U of Minnesota P, 1963.

13 THORNTON, Weldon. *Allusions in* Ulysses: *An Annotated List.* Chapel Hill: U of North Carolina P, 1968.

CRITICAL AND BIOGRAPHICAL BOOKS

14 ADAMS, Robert M. *Surface and Symbol: The Consistency of James Joyce's* Ulysses. New York: Oxford U P, 1962.*†

15 ADAMS, Robert M. *James Joyce: Common Sense and Beyond.* New York: Random House, 1966.*†

16 ATHERTON, J. S. *The Books at the Wake: A Study of Literary Allusions in James Joyce's* Finnegans Wake. New York: Viking, 1960.*

17 BECKETT, Samuel, and others. *Our Exagmination . . . of Work in Progress.* Norfolk, Conn.: New Directions, 1939.*

1 BENSTOCK, Bernard. *Joyce-Again's Wake: An Analysis of* Finnegans Wake. Seattle: U of Washington P, 1965.

2 BUDGEN, Frank. *James Joyce and the Making of* Ulysses. Bloomington: Indiana U P, 1960.*

3 BYRNE, J. F. *Silent Years: An Autobiography with Memoirs of James Joyce and Our Ireland.* New York: Farrar, Straus, and Giroux, 1953.

4 COLUM, Mary and Padraic. *Our Friend James Joyce.* Garden City, N.Y.: Doubleday, 1958.

5 DUJARDIN, Edouard. *Le monologue intérieur: Son apparition, ses origines, sa place dans l'oeuvre de James Joyce.* Paris: Messein, 1931.

6 ELLMANN, Richard. *James Joyce.* New York: Oxford U P, 1959. [Definitive biography.] *†

7 GILBERT, Stuart. *James Joyce's* Ulysses. London: Faber and Faber, 1930, rev. ed. 1952.

8 GOLDBERG, S. L. *The Classical Temper: A Study of James Joyce's* Ulysses. London: Chatto and Windus, 1961.*

9 GOLDMAN, Arnold. *The Joyce Paradox: Form and Freedom in His Fiction.* Evanston, Ill.: Northwestern U P, 1966.

10 HART, Clive. *Structure and Motif in* Finnegans Wake. London: Faber and Faber, 1962.*

11 HEALEY, George Harris, ed. *The Dublin Diary of Stanislaus Joyce.* London: Faber and Faber, 1962.

12 HIGGINSON, F. H. *Anna Livia Plurabelle: The Making of a Chapter.* Minneapolis: U of Minnesota P, 1960.

13 JOYCE, Stanislaus. *My Brother's Keeper.* Ed. Richard Ellmann. Preface by T. S. Eliot. New York: Viking, 1958.*

14 KAIN, Richard. *Fabulous Voyager.* Chicago: U of Chicago P, 1947; rev. ed., New York: Viking, 1959.

15 KENNER, Hugh. *Dublin's Joyce.* Bloomington: Indiana U P, 1956.*

16 LEVIN, Harry. *James Joyce: A Critical Introduction.* Norfolk, Conn.: New Directions, 1941; rev. ed., 1960.*†

17 LITZ, A. Walton. *The Art of James Joyce: Method and Design in* Ulysses *and* Finnegans Wake. London: Oxford U P, 1961; rev. ed., New York: Oxford U P, 1964.*†

18 MAGALANER, Marvin. *Time of Apprenticeship: The Fiction of Young James Joyce.* New York: Abelard-Schuman, 1959. [*Dubliners.*] *

19 MAGALANER, Marvin, and Richard KAIN. *Joyce: The Man, the Work, the Reputation.* New York: New York U P, 1956.

20 MORSE, J. Mitchell. *The Sympathetic Alien: Joyce and Catholicism.* New York: New York U P, 1959.

21 O'BRIEN, Darcy. *The Conscience of James Joyce.* Princeton: Princeton U P, 1968.

1 POUND, Ezra. *The Letters of Ezra Pound to James Joyce with Pound's Essay on Joyce.* Ed. and with commentary by Forrest Read. New York: New Directions, 1967.*†

2 PRESCOTT, Joseph. *Exploring James Joyce.* Preface by Harry T. Moore. Carbondale, Ill.: Southern Illinois U P, 1964.

3 STRONG, L. A. G. *The Sacred River: An Approach to James Joyce.* London: Methuen, 1949.

4 SULLIVAN, K. *Joyce Among the Jesuits.* New York: Columbia U P, 1958.

5 SULTAN, Stanley. *The Argument of* Ulysses. Columbus, Ohio: Ohio State U P, 1965.

6 TINDALL, William York. *James Joyce: His Way of Interpreting the Modern World.* New York: Scribner's, 1950.†

CRITICAL ESSAYS

A number of important essays not listed individually appear in the contents of the first nine titles, which are collections.

7 *James Joyce Quarterly.* Ed. Thomas Staley. University of Tulsa, Fall 1963- . [Reviews new criticism.]

8 CONNOLLY, Thomas E., ed. *Joyce's Portrait: Criticisms and Critiques.* New York: Appleton-Century-Crofts, 1962.

9 GIVENS, S., ed. *James Joyce: Two Decades of Criticism.* New York: Vanguard, 1948, 1963. [Contains a number of well known essays.] *

10 HART, Clive, ed. *James Joyce's* Dubliners: *Critical Essays.* London: Faber and Faber, 1969. [Fifteen essays, each on a story in *Dubliners.*]

11 JOLAS, Maria, ed. *A James Joyce Yearbook.* Paris: Transition, 1949. [Important for Continental opinion of Joyce.] *

12 MAGALANER, Marvin, ed. *A James Joyce Miscellany: Third Series.* Carbondale, Ill.: Southern Illinois U P, 1962.

13 MORRIS, William E., and Clifford A. NAULT, eds. *Portraits of an Artist.* New York: Odyssey, 1962.

14 SCHUETTE, William, ed. *Twentieth Century Interpretations of* A Portrait of the Artist as a Young Man. Englewood Cliffs, N.J.: Prentice-Hall, 1968.

15 STALEY, Thomas F., ed. *James Joyce Today: Essays on the Major Works.* Bloomington: Indiana U P, 1966.

16 BEEBE, Maurice. "Barnacle Goose and Lapwing." *PMLA* 71(1956):302-20.

17 BENSTOCK, Bernard. "L. Boom as Dreamer in *Finnegans Wake.*" *PMLA* 82(1967):91-7.

18 BLACKMUR, R. P. "The Jew in Search of a Son." *VQR* 24(1948):96-116.

1 BLOCK, Haskell M. "The Critical Theory of James Joyce." *JAAC* 8(1950): 172-84.*

2 BRISKEN, Irene Orgel. "Some New Light on 'The Parable of the Plums.' " *James Joyce Quarterly* 3,iv(1966):236-51.

3 BURGUM, E. B. See 13.7, "*Ulysses* and the Impasse of Individualism," pp. 95-108; "The Paradox of Skepticism in *Finnegans Wake*," pp. 109-19.

4 BUTOR, Michel. "Esquisse d'un seuil pour Finnegan." *Essais sur les modernes.* Paris: Gallimard, 1964, pp. 283-309.

5 CARRIER, Warren. "*Dubliners:* Joyce's Dantean Vision." *Ren* 17(1965): 211-5.

6 CHURCH, Margaret. "James Joyce: Time and Time Again." See 11.6, pp. 27-66.

7 COPE, J. I. "The Rhythmic Gesture: Image and Aesthetic in Joyce's *Ulysses.*" *ELH* 29(1962):67-89.

8 CURTIUS, E. R. "James Joyce und sein *Ulysses.*" *Kritische Essays zur Europaischen Literatur.* Bern: Francke, 1954, pp. 290-314.*

9 DAHLBERG, Edward, and Herbert READ. "On James Joyce." *Truth is More Sacred: A Critical Exchange on Modern Literature.* New York: Horizon, n.d., pp. 11-65.

10 DIBBLE, Brian. "A Brunonian Reading of Joyce's *A Portrait of the Artist.*" *James Joyce Quarterly* 4(1967):280-5.

11 DUNCAN, Edward. "Unsubstantial Father: A Study of the *Hamlet* Symbolism in Joyce's *Ulysses.*" *UTQ* 19(1950):126-40.

12 FESHBACH, Sidney. "A Slow and Dark Birth: A Study of the Organization of *A Portrait of the Artist as a Young Man.*" *James Joyce Quarterly* 4(1967):289-300.

13 FLEISHMAN, Avrom. "Science in Ithaca." *WSCL* 8(1967):377-91. [*Ulysses.*]

14 FRYE, Northrop. "Quest and Cycle in *Finnegans Wake.*" *JJR* 1(1957): 39-47.

15 GHISELIN, Brewster. "The Unity of Joyce's *Dubliners.*" *Accent* 16(1956): 75-88, 196-213.*

16 GIBBONS, T. H. "*Dubliners* and the Critics." *CritQ* 9(1967):179-87.

17 HARDY, Barbara. "Form as End and Means in *Ulysses.*" *OL* 19(1964): 194-200.

18 HAYMAN, David. "Forms of Folly in Joyce: A Study of Clowning in *Ulysses.*" *ELH* 34(1967):260-83.

19 HENDRY, Irene. "Joyce's Epiphanies." *SR* 54(1946):449-67. Repr. in 68.9, pp. 27-46.*

20 HODGART, M. J. C. "Work in Progress." *Cambridge Journal* 6(1952):23-39.

21 HOFFMAN, F. J. "Infroyce." See 4.17, pp. 114-48. Repr. in 68.9, pp. 390-435.*

1 HOWARTH, Herbert. "James Augustine Joyce." See 5.4, pp. 245-87. [Joyce and the Parnell legend.]

2 JUNG, C. J. "*Ulysses:* A Monologue." *Nimbus* 2,i(1953):7-20.

3 KAIN, Richard. "Problems of Interpreting Joycean Symbolism." *JGE* 17(1966):227-35.

4 KAPLAN, Harold. "Stoom: The Universal Comedy of James Joyce." *The Passive Voice: An Approach to Modern Fiction.* Athens, Ohio: Ohio U P, 1966, pp. 43-91.

5 KENNER, Hugh. "The *Portrait* in Perspective." See 68.9, pp. 132-74.*

6 KETTLE, Arnold. "James Joyce: *Ulysses.*" See 16.7, II, pp. 135-51.

7 KLAWITTER, Robert. "Henri Bergson and James Joyce's Fictional World." *Comparative Literature Studies* 3(1966):429-37.

8 KNIGHT, Douglas. "The Reading of *Ulysses.*" *ELH* 19(1952):64-80.

9 LARBAUD, Valéry. "James Joyce." *NRF* 18(April 1922):385-405. English trans., *Criterion* 1, i(October 1922):94-103.

10 LINK, Frederick M. "The Aesthetics of Stephen Dedalus." *PELL* 2(1966): 140-9.

11 MC LUHAN, Marshall. "James Joyce: Trivial and Quadrivial." *Thought* 28(Spring 1953):75-98.

12 MASON, Ellsworth. "Joyce's Categories." *SR* 61(1953):427-32.

13 MORE, Paul Elmer. "James Joyce." *American Review* 5(1935):129-57.

14 MORSE, J. Mitchell. "Augustine's Theodicy and Joyce's Aesthetics." *ELH* 24(March 1957):30-43.*

15 MORSE, J. Mitchell. "Karl Gutzkow and the Novel of Simultaneity." *James Joyce Quarterly* 2,i(1964):13-7.

16 NAREMORE, James. "Style as Meaning in *A Portrait of the Artist.*" *James Joyce Quarterly* 4(1967):331-42.

17 PETER, John. "Joyce and the Novel." *KR* 18(1956):619-32.

18 POSS, Stanley. "*Ulysses* and the Comedy of the Immobilized Act." *ELH* 24(March 1957):65-83.

19 POUND, Ezra. "James Joyce et Pécuchet." *Polite Essays*. London: Faber and Faber, 1937, pp. 82-97.

20 POWER, Arthur. "Conversations with Joyce." *James Joyce Quarterly* 3,i(1965):41-9.

21 REYNOLDS, Mary T. "Joyce and Nora: The Indispensable Countersign." *SR* 72(Winter 1964):29-64.

22 ROGERS, H. E. "Irish Myth and the Plot of *Ulysses.*" *ELH* 15(1948): 306-27.*

23 RUBIN, Louis D., Jr. "A Portrait of a Highly Visible Artist." *The Teller in the Tale.* Seattle: U of Washington P, 1967, pp. 141-77.

24 SCHLAUCH, Margaret. "The Language of James Joyce." *Science and Society* 3(1939):482-97. [*Finnegans Wake.*]

1 SCHOLES, Robert. "James Joyce, Irish Poet." *James Joyce Quarterly* 2(1965):255-70.

2 SCHOLES, Robert. "Joyce and the Epiphany: The Key to the Labyrinth?" *SR* 72(1964):65-77.*

3 SCHOLES, Robert. "Stephen Dedalus: *Eiron* and *Alazon.*" *TSLL* 3(1961): 8-15.

4 SPENCER, John. "A Note on the 'Steady Monologny of the Interiors.' " *REL* 6,ii(1965):32-41.

5 SPRINCHORN, Evert. "Joyce/A Portrait of the Artist as a Young Man: A Portrait of the Artist as Achilles." See 30.13, Unterecker, pp. 9-50.

6 STANFORD, W. B. *The Ulysses Theme: A Study in the Adaptability of a Traditional Hero.* Oxford: Blackwell, 1954, pp. 211-25.*

7 STEWART, J. I. M. "Joyce." See 6.4, pp. 422-83. Also bibliography, pp. 680-6.

8 THOMPSON, William Irwin. "The Language of *Finnegans Wake.*" *SR* 72(1964):78-90.

9 THRANE, James R. "Joyce's Sermon on Hell: Its Source and Its Backgrounds." *MP* 57(1960):172-98.*

10 TILLYARD, E. M. W. "Joyce: *Ulysses.*" See 12.21, pp. 187-96.

11 TINDALL, William York. "James Joyce and the Hermetic Tradition." *JHI* 15(1954):23-39.

12 TOYNBEE, Philip. "A Study of James Joyce's *Ulysses.*" See 68.9, pp. 243-84.*

13 TROY, William. "Stephen Dedalus and James Joyce." See 68.9, pp. 312-8.

14 WILSON, Edmund. "James Joyce." *Axel's Castle: A Study in the Imaginative Literature of 1870-1930.* New York: Scribner's, 1931, pp. 191-236. [A pioneer study.] * †

15 WILSON, Edmund. "The Dream of H. C. Earwicker." *The Wound and the Bow: Seven Studies in Literature.* New York: Oxford U P, 1947. Repr. in 68.9, pp. 319-42.*

D. (David) H. (Herbert) Lawrence (1885-1930)

TEXTS

There is no authoritative text of any of Lawrence's novels.

16 *The Phoenix Edition of D. H. Lawrence.* London: Heinemann, 1954- . [Includes novels, short novels, short stories, travel books, poems, plays, letters, and posthumous papers.]

17 *The Penguin D. H. Lawrence.* London: Penguin, 1950- . [Includes all the novels and short novels, as well as other works.]

1 *Lady Chatterley's Lover.* Introduction by Mark Schorer. New York: Grove, 1959. [Complete and unabridged, 3d manuscript version first published by Guiseppe Orioli, Florence, 1928.]

2 *Lady Chatterley's Lover.* Ed. C. H. Rolph. Introduction by Richard Hoggart. 2d ed. London: Penguin, 1961. [Heinemann has announced for publication, under the title *John Thomas and Lady Jane*, Lawrence's second draft of *Lady Chatterley's Lover*, previously unpublished.]

3 *Women in Love.* Foreword by Lawrence. New York: Random House, 1922, 1950. [On this text see Robert L. Chamberlain, 75.13]

4 *The Tales of D. H. Lawrence.* London: Secker, 1934.

5 *The Complete Poems of D. H. Lawrence.* Ed. With introduction and notes by Vivian de Sola Pinto and F. Warren Roberts. 2 vols. New York: Viking, 1964. [Definitive edition of his poems.]

6 *Psychoanalysis and the Unconscious and Fantasia of the Unconscious.* Introduction by Philip Rieff. New York: Viking, 1960.†

7 *Phoenix: The Posthumous Papers of D. H. Lawrence.* Ed. and with introduction by Edward D. McDonald. London: Heinemann, 1936; reissued, New York: Viking, 1968.*

8 *Phoenix II: Uncollected, Unpublished, and Other Prose Works by D. H. Lawrence.* Ed. with an introduction and notes by Harry T. Moore. New York: Viking, 1968.*

9 *Selected Literary Criticism.* Ed. Anthony Beal. London: Heinemann, 1956; London: Mercury, 1961.*†

10 *The Symbolic Meaning; The Uncollected Versions of Studies in Classic American Literature.* Ed. Armin Arnold. Preface by Harry T. Moore. New York: Viking, 1964.

11 *A D. H. Miscellany.* Ed. Harry T. Moore. Carbondale, Ill.: Southern Illinois U P, 1959.

12 TINDALL, William York, ed. *The Later D. H. Lawrence.* New York: Knopf, 1952. [Collection of Lawrence's later writings.]

13 TRILLING, Diana, ed. *The Portable D. H. Lawrence.* Introduction by Diana Trilling. New York: Viking, 1947.†

14 *The Letters of D. H. Lawrence.* Ed. Aldous Huxley. London: Heinemann, 1932.* [Important introduction.]

15 *Collected Letters of D. H. Lawrence.* 2 vols. Ed. Harry T. Moore. New York: Viking; London: Heinemann, 1962.*

16 TRILLING, Diana, ed. *Selected Letters of D. H. Lawrence.* Introduction by Diana Trilling. Garden City, N.Y.: Anchor, 1961.

BIBLIOGRAPHIES

17 BEEBE, Maurice, and Anthony TOMMASI. "Criticism of D. H. Lawrence: A Selected Checklist of Criticism with an Index to Studies of Separate Works." *MFS* 5,i(1959):83-98.*

18 POWELL, Lawrence Clark, ed. *The Manuscripts of D. H. Lawrence: A Descriptive Catalogue.* Foreword by Aldous Huxley. Los Angeles: The Public Library, 1937.

1 ROBERTS, F. Warren. *A Bibliography of D. H. Lawrence.* London: Hart-Davis, 1963.*

2 TANNENBAUM, Earl, ed. *D. H. Lawrence: An Exhibition of First Editions, Manuscripts, Paintings, Letters, and Miscellany.* Carbondale, Ill.: Southern Illinois U Library, 1958.

3 TEDLOCK, E. W., Jr. *The Frieda Lawrence Collection of D. H. Lawrence's Manuscripts: A Descriptive Bibliography.* Albuquerque: U of New Mexico P, 1948.

4 WHITE, W. *D. H. Lawrence: A Checklist 1931-1950.* Foreword by Frieda Lawrence. Detroit: Wayne State U P, 1950.*

CRITICAL AND BIOGRAPHICAL BOOKS

5 ALDINGTON, R. *Portrait of a Genius, But . . . : The Life of D. H. Lawrence.* London: Heinemann, 1950.*

6 CAVITCH, David. *D. H. Lawrence and the New World.* New York: Oxford U P, 1969.

7 CLARK, L. D. *Dark Night of the Body: D. H. Lawrence's* The Plumed Serpent. Austin: U of Texas P, 1964.

8 CORKE, Helen. *D. H. Lawrence: The Croydon Years.* Austin: U of Texas P, 1965.

9 COWAN, James C. *D. H. Lawrence's American Journey: A Study in Literature and Myth.* Cleveland: Case Western Reserve U P, 1971.

10 DALESKI, H. M. *The Forked Flame: A Study of D. H. Lawrence.* London: Faber and Faber, 1965.*

11 DRAPER, R. P., ed. *D. H. Lawrence: The Critical Heritage.* New York: Barnes and Noble, 1970.

12 "E. T." (Jessie Chambers). *D. H. Lawrence: A Personal Record.* London: Cape, 1935. 2d ed., ed. J. D. Chambers. New York: Barnes and Noble, 1965. [Information on Lawrence's early reading.] *

13 FORD, George H. *Double Measure: A Study of the Novels and Stories of D. H. Lawrence.* New York: Holt, Rinehart and Winston, 1965.

14 GOODHEART, Eugene. *The Utopian Vision of D. H. Lawrence.* Chicago: U of Chicago P, 1963.

15 GORDON, David J. *D. H. Lawrence as a Literary Critic.* New Haven: Yale U P, 1966.*

16 GREGORY, Horace. *D. H. Lawrence: Pilgrim of the Apocalypse, a Critical Study.* New York: Grove, 1957.

17 HOUGH, Graham. *The Dark Sun: A Study of D. H. Lawrence.* London: Duckworth, 1956.*

18 LAWRENCE, Frieda. *Not I, But the Wind.* London: Heinemann, 1934.

19 LAWRENCE, Frieda. *Frieda Lawrence: The Memoirs and Correspondence.* Ed. E. W. Tedlock, Jr. New York: Knopf, 1964.

1 LEAVIS, F. R. *D. H. Lawrence: Novelist.* London: Chatto and Windus, 1955. [A notable study, especially for *Women in Love.*] *†

2 MOORE, Harry T. *The Intelligent Heart: The Story of D. H. Lawrence.* London: Heinemann, 1955; rev. ed. 1960. [Standard biography.] *

3 MOORE, Harry T. *D. H. Lawrence: His Life and Works.* Rev. ed. New York: Twayne, 1964.

4 MOYNAHAN, Julian. *The Deed of Life.* Princeton: Princeton U P, 1963, 1966.*

5 MURRY, John Middleton. *Son of Woman: The Story of D. H. Lawrence.* London: Cape, 1931; 2d ed. 1954.

6 NEHLS, E. *D. H. Lawrence: A Composite Biography.* 3 vols. Madison: U of Wisconsin P, 1957-1959. [Direct commentary by Lawrence acquaintances.] *

7 SAGAR, Keith. *The Art of D. H. Lawrence.* Cambridge: Cambridge U P, 1966.

8 SPILKA, Mark. *The Love Ethic of D. H. Lawrence.* Bloomington: Indiana U P, 1955. [Includes bibliography.] *†

9 TALON, Henri A. *D. H. Lawrence:* Sons and Lovers, *les aspects socieux, le vision de l'artiste.* Paris: Lettres Modernes, 1965.

10 TEDLOCK, E. W., Jr. *D. H. Lawrence, Artist and Rebel: A Study of Lawrence's Fiction.* Albuquerque: U of New Mexico P, 1963.

11 TINDALL, William York. *D. H. Lawrence and Susan His Cow.* New York: Columbia U P, 1939, 1959.*

12 VIVAS, E. *D. H. Lawrence: The Failure and the Triumph of Art.* Evanston, Ill.: Northwestern U P, 1960.*†

13 WIDMER, Kingsley. *The Art of Perversity: D. H. Lawrence's Shorter Fictions.* Seattle: U of Washington P, 1962.*

14 YOUNG, Kenneth. *D. H. Lawrence.* London: Longmans, Green, 1952; rev. ed. 1960. [British Council pamphlet.]

CRITICAL ESSAYS

The first five titles are collections.

15 *The D. H. Lawrence Review.* Fayetteville, Ark.: U of Arkansas, 1968- [Published thrice yearly. Criticism, scholarship, reviews, bibliography.]

16 HOFFMAN, F. J., and H. T. MOORE, eds. *The Achievement of D. H. Lawrence.* Norman, Okla.: U of Oklahoma P, 1953.*

17 *MFS* 5,i(1959). Special Lawrence Issue.

18 SPILKA, Mark, ed. *D. H. Lawrence: A Collection of Critical Views.* Englewood Cliffs, N.J.: Prentice-Hall, 1963.

19 TEDLOCK, E. W., Jr., ed. *D. H. Lawrence and* Sons and Lovers*: Sources and Criticism.* New York: New York U P, 1965.*

20 ALEXANDER, John. "D. H. Lawrence's 'Kangaroo': Fantasy, Fact or Fiction?" *Meanjin* 24(1965):179-97.*

1 ALLOTT, Kenneth and Miriam. "D. H. Lawrence and Blanche Jennings." *REL* 1,iii(1960):57-76.

2 ARNOLD, Armin. "D. H. Lawrence, the Russians, and Giovanni Verga." *Comparative Literature Studies*, 2(1965):249-57.

3 AUDEN, W. H. "Some Notes on D. H. Lawrence." *Nation* 164(April 26, 1947):482.

4 AUDEN, W. H. "D. H. Lawrence." *The Dyer's Hand and Other Essays*. New York: Random House, 1962, pp. 277-95. [Mostly on poetry.] *

5 BEDIENT, Calvin. "The Radicalism of *Lady Chatterley's Lover*." *HudR* 19(1966):407-16.

6 BEEBE, Maurice. "Lawrence's Sacred Fount: The Artist Theme of *Sons and Lovers*." *TSLL* 4(1962):539-52.

7 BENTLEY, E. "D. H. Lawrence, John Thomas and Dionysos." *A Century of Hero Worship*. Philadelphia: Lippincott, 1944, pp. 231-53.

8 BLACKMUR, R. P. "D. H. Lawrence and Expressive Form." *Language as Gesture*. London: Allen and Unwin, 1961, pp. 286-300.*

9 BLISSETT, William. "D. H. Lawrence, D'Annunzio, Wagner." *WSCL* 7(1966):21-46.

10 BRAMLEY, J. A. "D. H. Lawrence and 'Miriam.'" *Cornhill Magazine* 171(1960):241-9.

11 BRANDA, Eldon S. "Textual Changes in *Women in Love*." *TSLL* 6(1964): 306-21.

12 CAUDWELL, C. "D. H. Lawrence: A Study of the Bourgeois Artist." *Studies in a Dying Culture*. New York: Dodd, Mead, 1938, pp. 44-72. [Marxist criticism.]†

13 CHAMBERLAIN, Robert L. "Pussum, Minette, and the Africo-Nordic Symbol in Lawrence's *Women in Love*." *PMLA* 78(1963):407-16.*

14 CLARK, L. D. "Lawrence, *Women in Love*: The Contravened Knot." See 30.13, Unterecker, pp. 51-78.

15 CORNWELL, Ethel F. See 13.9, pp. 208-41.

16 DAHLBERG, Edward, and Herbert READ. "On D. H. Lawrence." See 69.9, pp. 69-117.

17 DEAKIN, William. "D. H. Lawrence's Attacks on Proust and Joyce." *EIC* 7(1957):383-403.

18 DONALD, D. R. "The First and Final Versions of *Lady Chatterley's Lover*." *Theoria* 16-22(1964):85-97.

19 DRAPER, R. P. "Satire as a Form of Sympathy: D. H. Lawrence as Satirist." *Renaissance and Modern Essays*. Ed. G. R. Hibbard. London: Routledge and Paul, 1966, pp. 189-97.

20 DRAPER, R. P. "The Sense of Reality in the Work of D. H. Lawrence." *RLV* 33,v(1967):461-70.

1 ENGELBERG, Edward. "Escape from the Circles of Experience: D. H. Lawrence's *The Rainbow* as a Modern *Bildungsroman.*" *PMLA* 78(1963):103-13.

2 FORD, George H. "An Introductory Note to D. H. Lawrence's Prologue to *Women in Love.*" *TQ* 6,i(1963):92-7. [Precedes Lawrence's unpublished prologue, pp. 98-111.] *

3 FRAIBERG, Louis. "The Unattainable Self: D. H. Lawrence's *Sons and Lovers.*" See 29.20, Shapiro, pp. 175-201.

4 GOLDBERG, S. L. "*The Rainbow*: Fiddle-Bow and Sand." *EIC* 11(1961): 418-34.*

5 GORDON, David J. "D. H. Lawrence's Quarrel with Tragedy." *Per* 13(1964):135-50.*

6 GRAY, Ronald. *The German Tradition in Literature 1871-1945.* Cambridge: Cambridge U P, 1967, pp. 327-54.

7 GREGOR, Ian, and Brian NICHOLAS. "The Novel as Prophecy: *Lady Chatterley's Lover.*" See 14.3, pp. 217-48.

8 HASSALL, C. "D. H. Lawrence and the Etruscans." *EDH* 31(1962):61-78.*

9 HOFFMAN, F. J. "Lawrence's Quarrel with Freud." See 4.17, pp. 149-80.*

10 HOLBROOK, David. "The Fiery Hill: *Lady Chatterley's Lover.*" *The Quest for Love.* University, Ala.: U of Alabama P, 1965, pp. 192-333.

11 HUXLEY, Aldous. "Introduction." See 72.14, pp. ix-xxxiv.*

12 KAZIN, Alfred. "Sons, Lovers and Mothers." *PR* 29(1962):373-85.*

13 KERMODE, Frank. "Lawrence and the Apocalyptic Types." *CritQ* 9-10(1967-1968):14-38.

14 KETTLE, Arnold. "D. H. Lawrence: *The Rainbow.*" See 16.7, II, pp. 111-34.*

15 KNIGHT, G. Wilson. "Lawrence, Joyce, and Powys." *EIC* 11(1961):403-17.

16 LACHER, Walter. *L'amour et le divin.* Geneva: Gentil, 1961, pp. 63-102.

17 LE BRETON, Georges. "D. H. Lawrence et l'architecture du roman." *Preuves* 189(November 1966):70-3.

18 LERNER, Lawrence. *The Truthtellers: Jane Austen, George Eliot, D. H. Lawrence.* London: Chatto and Windus, 1967, pp. 172-235.

19 MARTIN, W. R. "'Freedom Together' in D. H. Lawrence's *Women in Love.*" *ESA* 8(1965):111-20.

20 MORI, Haruhide. "Lawrence's Imagistic Development in *The Rainbow* and *Women in Love.*" *ELH* 31(1964):460-81.*

21 MURRY, John Middleton. *Between Two Worlds: An Autobiography.* London: Cape, 1935, pp. 261-429 *passim.* [On his acquaintance with Lawrence.]

1 MYERS, Neil. "Lawrence and the War." *Criticism* 4,i(1962):44-58.

2 PANICHAS, George A. "D. H. Lawrence and the Ancient Greeks." *EM* 16(1965):195-214.

3 PANICHAS, George A. "F. M. Dostoevsky and D. H. Lawrence; Their Vision of Evil." *RMS* 5(1961):49-75.

4 PINTO, Vivian de Sola. "The Burning Bush: D. H. Lawrence as Religious Poet." *Mansions of the Spirit: Essays in Literature and Religion.* Ed. George Panichas. New York: Hawthorn, 1967, pp. 213-38.

5 PORTER, Katherine Anne. "A Wreath for the Gamekeeper." *Encounter* 14(February 1960):69-77. Repr. in *Encounters: An Anthology.* Ed. Stephen Spender, Irving Kristol, Melvin Lasky. New York: Basic Books, 1963, pp. 277-90.

6 RALEIGH, John Henry. "Victorian Morals and the Modern Novel." *PR* 25(1958):241-64.

7 ROBSON, W. W. "D. H. Lawrence and *Women in Love.*" See 8.3, Ford, pp. 280-300.

8 SHARPE, Michael C. "The Genesis of D. H. Lawrence's *The Trespasser.*" *EIC* 11(1961):34-9.

9 SPENDER, Stephen. "Notes on D. H. Lawrence." See 9.3, pp. 176-86.

10 SPENDER, Stephen. "Pioneering the Instinctive Life." See 9.2, pp. 92-107.*

11 STEWART, J. I. M. "Lawrence." See 6.4, pp. 484-593. [See also selected bibliography, pp. 686-95.] *

12 TEDLOCK, E. W., Jr. "D. H. Lawrence's Annotation of Ouspensky's *Tertium Organum.*" *TSLL* 2(1960):206-18.

13 TROY, William. "D. H. Lawrence as Hero." "The Lawrence Myth." *Selected Essays.* Ed. Stanley E. Hyman. New Brunswick: Rutgers U P, 1967, pp. 110-9, 120-33.

14 VICKERY, John B. "*The Plumed Serpent* and the Eternal Paradox." *Criticism* 5,ii(1963):119-34.

15 WILDE, Alan. "The Illusion of St. Mawr: Technique and Vision in D. H. Lawrence's Novel." *PMLA* 79(1964):164-70.

16 WILLIAMS, Raymond. "D. H. Lawrence." See 50.13, pp. 213-30.*

17 WILLIAMS, Raymond. "D. H. Lawrence." See 9.5, pp. 169-84.

18 WILLIAMS, Raymond. "Social and Personal Tragedy, Tolstoy and Lawrence." *Modern Tragedy.* London: Chatto and Windus, 1966, pp. 121-38.*

19 WOOLF, Virginia. "Notes on D. H. Lawrence." See 114.15, I, pp. 352-55.

78

(Percy) Wyndham Lewis (1882-1957)

TEXTS

1 *Tarr.* Rev. ed. London: Methuen, 1951.†

2 *The Revenge for Love.* London: Methuen; Chicago: Regnery, 1952.

3 *Self-Condemned.* London: Methuen, 1954. Chicago: Regnery, 1955.†

4 *The Human Age.* Introduction by Michael Ayrton. 3 vols. I: *The Childermass*, 1956. II: *Monstre Gai*, 1955. III: *Malign Fiesta*, 1955. London: Methuen, 1955-1956.

5 *The Childermass. Monstre Gai.* London: Calder, 1965. *Malign Fiesta.* London: Calder and Boyars, 1966.†

6 *The Apes of God.* Baltimore: Penguin, 1965.†

7 *Soldier of Humor: Selected Writings of Wyndham Lewis.* Ed. Raymond Rosenthal. New York: New American Library, 1966.†

8 *Time and Western Man.* Boston: Beacon, 1957.*†

9 *Men Without Art.* New York: Russell and Russell, 1965. [Criticism.]

10 *Wyndham Lewis the Artist, from* Blast *to Burlington House.* London: Laidlaw and Laidlaw, 1939. [Includes material from *Blast*, 1914, 1915.]

11 *Blasting and Bombardiering.* Berkeley: U of California P; London: Calder and Boyars, 1967. [Autobiographical.] *

12 *The Letters of Wyndham Lewis.* Ed. by W. K. Rose. London: Methuen; Norfolk, Conn.: New Directions, 1963.*

BIBLIOGRAPHIES

13 ROSE, W. K. *Wyndham Lewis at Cornell.* Ithaca, N.Y.: Cornell U P, 1961. [On the Lewis Archive at Cornell.]

14 TODD, Ruthven. "Check List of Books and Articles by Wyndham Lewis." *Twentieth-Century Verse*,9(March 1938):21-7.

15 WAGNER, Geoffrey. "Bibliography." See 79.5, pp. 315-48. [Part I, checklist of the writings of Lewis, pp. 315-36. Part II, secondary sources, pp. 336-48.] *

CRITICAL AND BIOGRAPHICAL BOOKS

16 GRIGSON, Geoffrey. *A Master of Our Time: A Study of Wyndham Lewis.* London: Methuen, 1951.*

17 HANDLEY-READ, C., ed. *The Art of Wyndham Lewis.* London: Faber and Faber, 1951. [Includes consideration of Lewis as visual artist.] *

1 KENNER, Hugh. *Wyndham Lewis.* Norfolk, Conn.: New Directions, 1954.*†

2 PRITCHARD, W. H. *Wyndham Lewis.* New York: Twayne, 1968.

3 ROBERTS, William. *The Resurrection of Vorticism and the Apotheosis of Wyndham Lewis at the Tate.* London: Favil, 1956.

4 TOMLIN, E. W. F. *Wyndham Lewis.* London: Longmans, Green, 1955. [British Council pamphlet.]

5 WAGNER, Geoffrey. *Wyndham Lewis: A Portrait of the Artist as the Enemy.* New Haven: Yale U P, 1957.*

CRITICAL ESSAYS
The first two titles are collections.

6 *Shen* 4,ii,iii(1953). Wyndham Lewis Number.

7 *Twentieth-Century Verse* 6/7(November/December 1937). Wyndham Lewis Double Number.

8 ALLEN, Walter. "Lonely Old Volcano: The Achievement of Wyndham Lewis." *Encounter* 21,iii(1963):63-70.*

9 CARTER, Thomas. "Rationalist in Hell." *KR* 18(1956):326-36. [On *The Human Age.*]

10 ELIOT, T. S. "Wyndham Lewis: Two Views." *Shen* 4,ii,iii(1953):65-71.*

11 ELIOT, T. S. "A Note on Monstre Gai." *HudR* 7(1955):522-6.

12 FJELDE, Rolf. "Time, Space, and Wyndham Lewis." *Western Review* 15,iii(1951):201-12. [On *Time and Western Man.*]

13 FRYE, Northrop. "Neo-Classical Agony." *HudR* (Winter 1957-1958):592-8.

14 HENDERSON, Philip. "Wyndham Lewis and the Function of Satire." See 8.9, pp. 97-102.

15 HOLLOWAY, John. "Wyndham Lewis: The Massacre and the Innocents." *The Charted Mirror.* London: Routledge and Paul, 1960, pp. 118-36.*

16 KENNER, Hugh. "The Devil and Wyndham Lewis." *Gnomon.* New York: McDowell-Obolensky, 1958, pp. 215-41.*

17 KIRK, Russell. "Wyndham Lewis's First Principles." *YR* 44(1955):520-34.

18 MC LUHAN, Marshall. "Wyndham Lewis: His Theory of Art and Communication." *Shen* 4,ii,iii(1953):77-88.

19 MUDRICK, M. "The Double-Artist and the Injured Party." *Shen* 4,ii,iii (1953):54-64.

20 POUND, Ezra. "Vorticism." *Fortnightly Review* 102(September 1914): 461-71.*

1 POUND, Ezra. "Augment of the Novel." *New Directions in Prose and Poetry 6.* Norfolk, Conn.: New Directions, 1941, pp. 705-13. [On *The Apes of God.*]

2 PRITCHETT, V. S. "The Eye-Man." See 37.6, pp. 248-53.

3 ROTHENSTEIN, John. "Wyndham Lewis, 1882-1957." *Sickert to Grant.* Vol. I of *Modern English Painters.* London: Arcon Books, 1962, pp. 276-312.

4 SEYMOUR-SMITH, Martin. "Zero and the Impossible." *Encounter* 9(November 1957):41-5.

5 SPENDER, Stephen. "The Great Without." See 9.3, pp. 204-16.*

6 STONIER, George Walter. "Wyndham Lewis." *Gog Magog and Other Critical Essays.* London: Dent, 1933, pp. 88-95.

7 WAGNER, Geoffrey. "Wyndham Lewis and James Joyce: A Study in Controversy." *SAQ* 56(January 1957):57-66.*

8 WIEBE, Dallas E. "Wyndham Lewis and the Picaresque Novel." *SAQ* 62(1963):587-96.*

Rose Macaulay (1889-1958)

TEXTS

9 The Collected Edition. London: Collins, 1965- .

10 *They Were Defeated.* Introduction by C. V. Wedgewood. New ed. London: Collins, 1960.

11 *Told by an Idiot.* Introduction by Raymond Mortimer. London: Collins, 1965.

12 *The Towers of Trebizond.* New York: Farrar, Straus and Giroux, 1956; London: Collins, 1956, 1965.

13 *Pleasures of Ruins.* Ed. Constance Babington Smith. Interpreted in photographs by Roloff Beny. London: Thames and Hudson, 1965.

14 *Letters to a Friend 1950-1952.* Ed. Constance Babington Smith. London: Collins, 1961.

15 *Last Letters to a Friend 1952-1958.* Ed. Constance Babington Smith. London: Collins, 1962. New York: Atheneum, 1963.

16 *Letters to a Sister.* Ed. Constance Babington Smith. London: Collins, 1964.

BIBLIOGRAPHIES

There is no complete bibliography. *ELT* has published bibliographical items since 1957.

CRITICAL BOOKS
There are no critical books.

CRITICAL ESSAYS

1 BENSEN, Alice R. "The Skeptical Balance: A Study of Rose Macaulay's *Going Abroad.*" *PMASAL* 48(1963):675-83.

2 BENSEN, Alice R. "The Ironic Aesthete and the Sponsoring Causes: A Rhetorical Quandary in Novelistic Technique." *ELT* 9,i(1966):39-43.

3 BURGESS, Anthony. "The Pattern and the Core." *Spectator* 215(July 2, 1965):20, 22.*

4 CHASE, Mary Ellen. "Five Literary Portraits." *MR* 3(1962):511-6.

5 DALGLISH, Doris. "Some Contemporary Women Novelists." *Contemporary Review* 127:82(January 1925):78-85.

6 ELLIS, G. V. See 8.1, pp. 101, 194, 201, 352-6.

7 INGLISHAM, John. "Rose Macaulay." *Bookman* 72(1927):107-10.

8 IRWIN, W. R. "Permanence and Change in *The Edwardians* and *Told by an Idiot.*" *MFS* 2(1956):63-7.

9 KLUGE, Margaret. "Die Stellung Rose Macaulays zur Frau." *Anglia. Zeitschrift für Englische Philologie* 52(June 1928):136-74.

10 LOCKWOOD, William J. "Rose Macaulay." *Minor British Novelists.* Ed. Charles Alva Hoyt. Carbondale, Ill.: Southern Illinois U P, 1967, pp. 135-56.*

11 STEWART, Douglas. "Rose Macaulay–Anglicanism." *The Ark of God: Studies in Five Modern Novelists.* London: Kingsgate, 1961, pp. 99-128.

12 SWINNERTON, Frank. "Rose Macaulay." *Spectator* 184(1950):653.

W. (William) Somerset Maugham (1874-1965)

TEXTS

13 *The Collected Edition of the Works of W. Somerset Maugham.* London: Heinemann. [Begun in 1931 with selected plays, followed at intervals by novels, short stories, and travel books. Prefaces to each volume of plays and to early volumes of nondramatic works have biographical and bibliographical importance. Definitive but not complete edition.]

14 *The Complete Short Stories of W. Somerset Maugham.* 3 vols. London: Heinemann, 1951. [Definitive edition. Each volume has preface by Maugham.]

1 *The Selected Novels of W. Somerset Maugham.* 3 vols. London: Heinemann, 1953. [New preface to each volume.]

2 *Of Human Bondage.* New York: Modern Library, 1915. With introduction by Maugham, 1956.

3 *The Maugham Reader.* Introduction by Glenway Wescott. Garden City, N.Y.: Doubleday, 1950.

4 *A Maugham Twelve.* Stories selected with an introduction by Angus Wilson. London: Heinemann, 1966.

5 *Selected Prefaces and Introductions of W. Somerset Maugham.* Garden City, N.Y.: Doubleday, 1963.

6 *The Partial View.* London: Heinemann, 1954. [Contains autobiographical works *The Summing Up* and *A Writer's Notebook* with new preface by Maugham.] *

7 "*Of Human Bondage*, with A Digression on the Art of Fiction." Washington, D.C.: U. S. Government Printing Office, 1946. [An address by Maugham on presenting the original manuscript to the Library of Congress.]

BIBLIOGRAPHIES

8 *ELT* 1957- . [See especially 1,i(1957):30-2 and 6,iii(1963):108-17.] *

9 SANDERS, Charles. *W. Somerset Maugham: An Annotated Bibliography of Writings About Him.* De Kalb, Ill.: Northern Illinois U P, 1970.

10 STOTT, Raymond Toole. *The Writings of William Somerset Maugham: A Bibliography.* London: Rota, 1956; Supplement, 1961.*

CRITICAL AND BIOGRAPHICAL BOOKS

11 BRANDER, L. *Somerset Maugham: A Guide.* Edinburgh: Oliver and Boyd, 1963.*

12 BROPHY, John. *Somerset Maugham* London: Longmans, Green, 1952. [British Council pamphlet. Selected bibliography.] *

13 CORDELL, Richard A. *W. Somerset Maugham.* New York: Nelson, 1937; rev. ed. Bloomington: Indiana U P, 1961.

14 DOTTIN, Paul. *W. Somerset Maugham et ses romans.* Paris: Perrin, 1928.

15 GUERY, Suzanne. *La philosophie de Somerset Maugham.* Paris: Editions de France, 1933.

16 PAPAJEWSKI, Helmut. *Die Welt-, Lebens-, une Kunstanschauung William Somerset Maughams.* Köln: Kölner Universitäts-Verlag, 1952.*

CRITICAL ESSAYS

The first two titles are collections.

1 JONAS, Klaus W., ed. *The Maugham Enigma.* New York: Citadel, 1954. [An anthology of articles on Maugham and his works.] *

2 JONAS, Klaus W., ed. *The World of Somerset Maugham.* New York: British Book Centre, 1959. [Contains prefaces by Maugham and articles about Maugham.]

3 BASON, Fred T. "Mr. Somerset Maugham." *The Saturday Book.* Fifth year. Ed. Leonard Russell. London: Hutchinson, 1943, pp. 279-84.

4 CONNOLLY, Cyril. "The Art of Being Good." *The Condemned Playground.* New York: Macmillan, 1946, pp. 250-9.*

5 DOBRINSKY, V. "Aspects biographiques de l'oeuvre de Somerset Maugham: L'enfance." *EA* 8(1955):299-312.

6 GORDON, Caroline. "Notes on Chekhov and Maugham." *SR* 57(1949): 401-10.

7 HEYWOOD, C. "Two Printed Texts of Somerset Maugham's *Mrs. Craddock.*" *ELN* 5(1966):39-46.

8 KRIM, Seymour. "Maugham the Artist." *Cweal* 61(1954):284-7.

9 LAS VERGNAS, Raymond. "Somerset Maugham." *RDM* (January 15, 1966):171-80.

10 PAUL, David. "Maugham and Two Myths: Shown in *The Moon and Sixpence* and *The Razor's Edge.*" *Cornhill* 162(Autumn 1946):143-8.

11 POLLOCK, John. "Somerset Maugham and His Work." *QR* 304(1966): 365-78.

12 REDLIN, Rosemarie. "Somerset Maugham: *On a Chinese Screen.*" *NS* 13(1964):573-81.

13 ROSS, Woodburn O. "W. Somerset Maugham: Theme and Variations." *CE* 8(1946):113-22.*

14 ROUTH, H. V. See 5.15, pp. 146-53.

15 SPENCE, Robert. "Maugham's *Of Human Bondage:* The Making of a Masterpiece." *LC* 17,ii(1951):104-14.*

16 SPENCER, Theodore. "Somerset Maugham." *CE* 2(1940):1-10.*

17 WESCOTT, Glenway. "Somerset Maugham and Posterity." *Images of Truth: Remembrances and Criticism.* New York: Harper and Row, 1962, pp. 59-85.*

18 ZLOBINA, Maya. "The Surprises in Somerset Maugham." *SovR* 3,vi(1962): 3-9.

George Moore (1852-1933)

TEXTS

19 *The Works of George Moore.* Uniform Edition. London: Heinemann, 1927-1933. [Incomplete.] *

1 *The Works of George Moore.* Ebury Edition. 20 vols. London: Heinemann, 1937.

2 *The Collected Works of George Moore.* Carra Edition. 21 vols. New York: Boni and Liveright, 1922-1924.

3 *Esther Waters: A Novel.* With an Introduction and Textual Analysis. Ed. Lionel Stevenson. Boston: Houghton Mifflin, 1963.†

4 *Esther Waters.* Introduction by Walter Allen. London: Dent, 1962. [Everyman Ed.]

5 *Esther Waters.* Introduction by Graham Hough. London: Oxford U P, 1964.†

6 *Confessions of a Young Man.* Ed. and annotated by Moore, 1904 and 1916. Introduction by Robert M. Coates. New York: Capricorn, 1959.

7 *A Story-Teller's Holiday.* Preface by Ernest Longworth. New York: Liveright, 1929. [Black and Gold Library.]

8 *Memoirs of My Dead Life.* New York: Walker-de-Berry, 1960. [Boar's Head Book.]

9 *Letters from George Moore to E. Dujardin.* Trans. J. Eglinton. New York: Gaige, 1929.

10 *Letters of George Moore.* Introduction by John Eglinton, to whom they were written. Bournemouth: Sydenham, 1942.

11 *George Moore in Transition: Letters to T. Fisher Unwin and Lena Milman, 1894-1910.* Ed. Helmut E. Gerber. Detroit: Wayne State U P, 1968.*

12 *George Moore: Letters to Lady Cunard.* Ed. Rupert Hart-Davis. London: Hart-Davis, 1957.*

BIBLIOGRAPHIES

13 GERBER, Helmut E. *George Moore: An Annotated Bibliography of Writings About Him.* West Lafayette, Ind.: English Department, Purdue U, 1959. [Contains the bibliography in *ELT* 2,ii(1959):1-91.] *

14 GILCHER, Edwin. *A Bibliography of George Moore.* De Kalb: Northern Illinois U P, 1970.

15 KORG, Jacob. "George Moore." See 48.14, Stevenson, pp. 389-401. [Selected and annotated.] *

CRITICAL AND BIOGRAPHICAL BOOKS

16 BROWN, Malcolm. *George Moore: A Reconsideration.* Seattle: U of Washington P, 1955.*

17 COLLET, Georges-Paul. *George Moore et la France.* Geneva: Droz, 1957.*

1 CUNARD, Nancy. *G.M.: Memories of George Moore.* London: Hart-Davis, 1956.

2 FREEMAN, John. *A Portrait of George Moore in a Study of His Work.* London: Laurie, 1922. [Contains bibliography, 1878-1921, by H. Danielson, pp. 235-83.] *

3 GOODWIN, Geraint. *Conversations with George Moore.* New York: Knopf, 1930.

4 HONE, Joseph. *The Life of George Moore.* New York: Macmillan, 1936. [Standard biography.] *

5 JEFFARES, A. Norman. *George Moore.* London: Longmans, Green, 1965. [British Council pamphlet. Contains selected bibliography.] *

6 MORGAN, Charles. *An Epitaph on George Moore.* New York: Macmillan, 1935.

7 NOEL, Jean C. *George Moore: L'homme et l'oeuvre (1852-1933).* Paris: Didier, 1966.

CRITICAL ESSAYS

8 BAKER, E. A. See 7.2, IX, pp. 161-202.*

9 BAYLEN, Joseph. "George Moore, W. T. Stead, and the Boer War." *UMSE* 3(1962):49-60.

10 BENNETT, Arnold. "Mr. George Moore." *Fame and Fiction.* London: Richards, 1901, pp. 233-68.

11 BLISSETT, William. "George Moore and Literary Wagnerism." *CL* 13(Winter 1961):52-71.

12 BOWRA, C. M. "George Moore." *New Oxford Outlook* 1(May 1933):43-51.

13 CAZAMIAN, Madeleine. See 4.9, pp. 369-405 and *passim.**

14 CLARK, Barrett H. "George Moore." *Intimate Portraits.* New York: Dramatists Play Service, 1951, pp. 57-153.

15 COOPER, Douglas. "George Moore and Modern Art." *Horizon* 14(February 1945):113-30.

16 CORDASCO, Francesco. "G. Moore and E. Dujardin." *MLN* 62(April 1947): 244-51.

17 ELWIN, Malcolm. *Old Gods Falling.* New York: Macmillan, 1939, pp. 46-106.

18 FARMER, Albert J. "George Moore et les influences françaises." *Le mouvement esthétique et "decadent" en Angleterre (1879-1900).* Paris: Champion, 1931, pp. 76-120 and *passim.**

19 FRIERSON, William C. "George Moore, Naturalist." See 8.6, pp. 60-84.

20 GETTMAN, Royal. "George Moore's Revisions of *The Lake, The Wild Goose,* and *Esther Waters.*" *PMLA* 59(1944):540-55.*

1 GREGOR, Ian, and Brian NICHOLAS. "The Case of *Esther Waters.*" See 14.3, pp. 98-122.

2 GWYNN, Denis. *Edward Martyn and the Irish Revival.* London: Cape, 1930, pp. 13-38; 113-70.

3 HOUGH, Graham. "George Moore and the Novel." *REL* 1,i(1960):35-44. Also in 29.3, pp. 200-10.*

4 HOUGH, Graham. "George Moore and the Nineties." See 29.3, pp. 179-99.

5 HOWARTH, Herbert. "George Augustus Moore." See 5.4, pp. 32-82.

6 HUNEKER, James. "George Moore." *Overtones: A Book of Temperaments.* New York: Scribner's, 1904, pp. 188-213.

7 HUNEKER, James. "The Later George Moore." *The Pathos of Distance.* New York: Scribner's, 1913, pp. 16-48.

8 MC GREEVY, T. "George Moore." *Scrutinies.* See 46.6, Rickword, pp. 110-30.

9 OLIVERO, Federico. "George Moore." *Revue Germanique* 6(1910):166-73.*

10 PHELPS, Gilbert. See 5.14, pp. 96-109, 144-5, 157-8, and *passim.*

11 REID, Forrest. "The Novels of George Moore." *Westminster Review* 172(1909):200-8.

12 SCHWAB, Arnold T. "Irish Author and American Critic: George Moore and James Huneker." *NCF* 8(1954):256-71; 9(1954):22-37.

13 SHUMAKER, Wayne. "The Narrative Mode: Moore's *Hail and Farewell.*" *English Autobiography: Its Emergence, Materials, and Form.* Berkeley: U of California P, 1954, pp. 185-213. [U of California Publications, English Studies No. 8.]

14 STEWARD, S. M. "J. K. Huysmans and G. Moore." *RR* 25(July-September 1934):197-206.

15 YEATS, W. B. *The Autobiography of William Butler Yeats.* New York: Macmillan, 1953, especially pp. 243-6, 250-3, 258-72.

Charles Morgan (1894-1958)

TEXTS

16 *Collected Works.* London: Macmillan.

17 *The Fountain.* New York: Knopf, 1932, 1958.

18 *Portrait in a Mirror.* New York: St. Martin's P, 1957.

1 *The Writer and His World: Lectures and Essays.* London: Macmillan, 1960. [Contains 14 essays, several on literary topics.]

2 *Selected Letters of Charles Morgan.* Ed. and with a memoir by Eiluned Lewis. London: Macmillan, 1967.*

BIBLIOGRAPHIES

There is no separate bibliography.

CRITICAL AND BIOGRAPHICAL BOOKS

3 DE PANGE, Victor. *Charles Morgan.* Paris: Editions Universitaires, 1962.

4 DUFFIN, Henry Charles. *The Novels and Plays of Charles Morgan.* London: Bowes and Bowes, 1959.*

5 IKLE, Charlotte. *Individualität und Transzendenz bei Charles Morgan.* Zurich: Pieda, 1961.

CRITICAL ESSAYS

6 BONNEROT, Louis. "Essai sur les romans de Mr. Charles Morgan." *Revue anglo-américaine* 10(1932-1933):123-36.

7 DANE, Clemence. "*The River Line* (Personal Preference)." *TLS* (August 6, 1954):xxvi-xxvii.

8 GILLET, Louis. "Un romancier anglais, M. Charles Morgan." *RDM* 16 (1935):203-14.

9 GUYARD, M. F. "Charles Morgan en France." *RLC* 23(1949):71-9.*

10 HARDING, Joan. "Charles Morgan and the Metaphysic of Evil." *CR* 198 (1960):638-42.*

11 LACHER, Walter. "Charles Morgan." *L'amour et le divin.* Geneva: Gentil, 1961, pp. 103-52.*

12 LEWIS, Eiluned. "A Memoir." See 87.2, pp. 1-41.* [Biographical information on Morgan.]

13 MADAULE, Jacques. "Charles Morgan, ou la recherche du paradis perdu." *Esprit* 7(June 1939):374-95.

14 MAGNY, Claude-Edmonde. "Charles Morgan ou la servitude du charnel." *Les sandales d'Empédocle: Essai sur les limites de la littérature.* Boudry: Editions de la Baconnière, 1945, pp. 41-103.*

15 RIESNER, Dieter. "Charles Morgan: *Portrait in a Mirror.*" See 16.9, Oppel, pp. 222-44.*

Iris Murdoch (1919-)

TEXTS

Many Murdoch novels have appeared in paperback; for example, since 1960 the series in Penguin Books, Harmondsworth, England, in association with Chatto and Windus.

1 "The Novelist as Metaphysician." *Listener* 43(March 16, 1950):473, 476. [Deals with French "phenomenological novel."]

2 "The Sublime and the Good." *ChiR* 13,v(1959):42-55.

3 "Against Dryness: A Polemical Sketch." *Encounter* 16(1961):16-20. [The novel and character.]

4 "The Idea of Perfection." *YR* 53(March 1964):342-80.

5 *Sartre: Romantic Rationalist.* London: Bowes and Bowes, 1953, 1965. New Haven: Yale U P, 1961, 1969.

6 *The Sovereignty of Good.* London: Routledge and Paul, 1970. [Three papers on moral philosophy.]

BIBLIOGRAPHIES

7 CIVIN, Laraine. *Iris Murdoch: A Bibliography.* Johannesburg: U of Witwatersrand, Department of Bibliography, Librarianship, and Typography, 1968. [Records all writings published in English by and about Murdoch from May, 1941, to the end of January, 1968.]

8 WIDMANN, R. L. "An Iris Murdoch Checklist." *Crit* 10,i(1968):17-29.

CRITICAL AND BIOGRAPHICAL BOOKS

9 BYATT, Antonia S. *Degrees of Freedom: The Novels of Iris Murdoch.* London: Chatto and Windus, 1965.

10 RABINOVITZ, Rubin. *Iris Murdoch.* New York: Columbia U P, 1968. [Columbia Essays in Modern Writers.]

11 WOLFE, Peter. *The Disciplined Heart: Iris Murdoch and Her Novels.* Columbia, Mo.: U of Missouri P, 1966.

CRITICAL ESSAYS

12 BALDANZA, Frank. "Iris Murdoch and the Theory of Personality." *Criticism* 7(1965):176-89.

13 BRADBURY, Malcolm. "Iris Murdoch's *Under the Net.*" *CritQ* 4(1962):47-54.

14 BRUGIERE, Bernard. "L'univers romanesque d'Iris Murdoch." *MdF* 352 (1964):699-711.

1 DICK, Bernard F. "The Novels of Iris Murdoch: A Formula for Enchantment." *BuR* 14,ii(1966):66-81.

2 FELHEIM, Marvin. "Symbolic Characterization in the Novels of Iris Murdoch." *TSLL* 2(1960):189-97.

3 FRASER, G. S. "Iris Murdoch: The Solidity of the Normal." *International Literary Annual*, no. 2. Ed. John Wain. London: Calder, 1959, pp. 37-54.

4 GINDIN, James. "Images of Illusion in the Works of Iris Murdoch." *TSLL* 2(1960):180-8. Also in 16.1, pp. 178-95.

5 HALL, James. "Blurring the Will: The Growth of Iris Murdoch." *ELH* 32(1965):256-73. Also in 20.1, pp. 181-212.

6 HOFFMAN, F. J. "Iris Murdoch: The Reality of Persons." *Crit* 7(1964):48-57.

7 JONES, Dorothy. "Love and Morality in Irish Murdoch's *The Bell.*" *Meanjin* 26(1967):85-90.

8 KAEHELE, Sharon, and Howard GERMAN. "The Discovery of Reality in Iris Murdoch's *The Bell.*" *PMLA* 82(1967):554-63.

9 KERMODE, Frank. "The House of Fiction: Interviews with Seven English Novelists." *PR* 30(1963):62-5.

10 MC CABE, Bernard. "Guises of Love." *CWeal* 83(1965):270-3.

11 MARTIN, Graham. "Iris Murdoch and the Symbolist Novel." *BJA* 5(1965): 296-300.

12 MICHA, René. "Les romans à machines d'Iris Murdoch." *Critique* (Paris) 16,no.155(1960):291-301.

13 MORRELL, Roy. "Iris Murdoch: The Early Novels." *CritQ* 9(1967):272-82.

14 O'CONNOR, William Van. "Iris Murdoch: The Formal and the Contingent." *Crit* 3,ii(1960):34-46. Also in 5.13, pp. 54-74.

15 O'SULLIVAN, Kevin. "Iris Murdoch and the Image of Liberal Man." *Yale Literary Magazine* 131,ii(1962):27-36.

16 ROSE, W. K. "An Interview with Iris Murdoch." *Shen* 19,ii(1968):3-22.

17 SCHOLES, Robert. "Iris Murdoch's 'Unicorn.' " *The Fabulators.* New York: Oxford U P, 1967, pp. 106-32.

18 SOUVAGE, Jacques. "Symbol as Narrative Device: An Interpretation of Iris Murdoch's *The Bell.*" *ES* 43(1962):81-96.

19 SOUVAGE, Jacques. "Theme and Structure in Iris Murdoch's *The Flight from the Enchanter.*" *Spieghel Historiael van de Bond van Gentste Germanisten* 3(1960-1961):73-88.

20 SOUVAGE, Jacques. "The Unresolved Tension: An Interpretation of Iris Murdoch's *Under the Net.*" *RLV* 26(1960):420-30.

1 WALL, Stephen. "The Bell in *The Bell.*" *EIC* 13(1963):265-73.

2 WHITESIDE, George. "The Novels of Iris Murdoch." *Crit* 7(1964):27-47.

3 WIDMANN, R. L. "Murdoch's *Under the Net*: Theory and Practice of Fiction." *Crit* 10,i(1968):5-16.

L. (Leo) H. (Hamilton) Myers (1881-1944)

TEXTS

4 *The Near and the Far*, containing *The Root and the Flower* and *The Pool of Vishnu.* Introduction by L. P. Hartley. London: Cape, 1943, 1946, 1956.

BIBLIOGRAPHIES
There is no separate bibliography.

CRITICAL AND BIOGRAPHICAL BOOKS

5 BANTOCK, G. H. *L. H. Myers: A Critical Study.* London: Cape, 1956.*

CRITICAL ESSAYS

6 ALLEN, Walter. "L. H. Myers: A Personal Impression." *Orion: A Miscellany.* London: Nicholson and Watson, 1945, I, pp. 71-5.*

7 ALLEN, Walter. See 7.10, pp. 56-8.

8 BANTOCK, G. H. "L. H. Myers and Bloomsbury." See 8.3, Ford, pp. 270-9.

9 BANTOCK, G. H. "The Novels of L. H. Myers." See 16.12, Rajan, pp. 57-75.*

10 BOTTRALL, Ronald. "L. H. Myers." *REL* 2,ii(1961):47-58.*

11 EATON, Gai. "Mask and Man: L. H. Myers." *The Richest Vein: Eastern Tradition and Modern Thought.* London: Faber and Faber, 1949, pp. 146-65.

12 HARDING, D. W. "L. H. Myers." *Scrutiny* 4(1935):79-81.

13 HARTLEY, L. P. "The Near and the Far." See 58.13, pp. 143-8.*

14 WILSON, Colin. "L. H. Myers." *Eagle and Earwig.* London: Baker, 1965, pp. 171-90.

Liam O'Flaherty (1897-)

TEXTS

1 *The Informer.* Afterword by Donagh MacDonagh. New York: New American Library, 1961.

2 *Selected Stories.* Ed. Devin A. Garrity. New York: New American Library, 1958.

BIBLIOGRAPHIES

3 DOYLE, P. A., ed. "A Liam O'Flaherty Checklist." *TCL* 13(1967):49-51.*

4 GAWSWORTH, John, ed. "Liam O'Flaherty." *Ten Contemporaries: Notes Toward Their Definitive Bibliography.* Second series. London: Joiner and Steele, 1933, pp. 139-43. [Bibliography of O'Flaherty works. Autobiographical note by O'Flaherty, pp. 144-60.]

5 MILLETT, Fred B. "Liam O'Flaherty." See 3.18, pp. 400-2.*

CRITICAL BOOKS

6 ZNEIMER, John. *The Literary Vision of Liam O'Flaherty.* Syracuse: Syracuse U P, 1970.

CRITICAL ESSAYS

7 *The Irish Statesman.* For contemporary reviews of works by O'Flaherty see 7(1926):279-80; 8(1927):304; 10(1928):295; 13(1929):76.

8 KELLEHER, John B. "Irish Literature Today." *Atlantic Monthly* 175(1945):70-6.

9 KIELY, Benedict. See 8.12.

10 KUNITZ, Stanley J., and Howard HAYCRAFT, eds. See 3.15, First Supplement, 1955, pp. 734-5.

11 MERCIER, Vivian. "Man Against Nature: The Novels of Liam O'Flaherty." *Wascana Review* 1,iii(1966):37-46.

12 O'FAOLAIN, Sean. "Don Quixote O'Flaherty." *London Mercury* 37(1937): 170-5.

13 O'FAOLAIN, Sean. "Liam O'Flaherty." *Writers of Today 2.* Ed. Denys Val Baker. London: Sidgwick and Jackson, 1948, pp. 167-76.*

14 PAUL-DUBOIS, L. "Un romancier réaliste en Erin." *RDM* 21(1934):884-904.

15 PRITCHETT, V. S. *New Statesman and Nation* 4(1932):103. [Review of *Skerrett.*]

1 SAUL, George B. "A Wild Sowing: The Short Stories of Liam O'Flaherty." *REL* 4,iii(1963):108-13.*

2 TROY, William. "The Position of Liam O'Flaherty." *Bookman* (New York) 69(March 1929):7-11.*

3 WARREN, C. H. "Liam O'Flaherty." *Bookman*(London) 77(January 1930): 235-6.

4 YEATS, W. B. *The Letters of W. B. Yeats.* Ed. Allan Wade. London: Hart-Davis, 1954, pp. 722, 801, 809. [Comments on O'Flaherty novels.]

George Orwell (pseud. Eric Arthur Blair) (1903-1950)

TEXTS

All of the novels and several nonfictional works are available in paperback.

5 *Works.* Uniform Edition. London: Secker and Warburg, 1948- . [Includes all the novels and some nonfictional works.]

6 *Orwell's* Nineteen Eighty-Four*: Text, Sources, Criticism.* Ed. Irving Howe. New York: Harcourt, Brace and World, 1963. [Contains bibliography.]

7 *The Orwell Reader: Fiction, Essays and Reportage by George Orwell.* Ed. Richard Rovere. New York: Harcourt, Brace, 1956.†

8 *Homage to Catalonia.* Introduction by Lionel Trilling. New York: Harcourt, Brace, 1952. Boston: Beacon, 1955.*†

9 *The Road to Wigan Pier.* Foreword by Victor Gollancz. New York: Harcourt, Brace, 1958.

10 *Collected Essays.* London: Secker and Warburg, 1961.

11 ORWELL, Sonia, and Ian ANGUS, eds. *The Collected Essays, Journalism and Letters of George Orwell.* 4 vols. New York: Harcourt, Brace, 1968.

BIBLIOGRAPHIES

12 MC DOWELL, Jennifer. "George Orwell: Bibliographical Addenda." *BB* 23(January-April 1963):224-9; 24(May-August 1963):19-24; 24(September-December 1963):36-40.*

13 WILLISON, I. R., and Ian ANGUS. "George Orwell: Bibliographical Addenda." *BB* 24(September-December 1965):180-7.

14 ZEKE, Zoltang, and W. WHITE. "George Orwell–A Selected Bibliography." *BB* 23(May-August 1961):110-4.*

15 ZEKE, Zoltang, and W. WHITE. "Orwelliana: A Checklist." *BB* 23(September-December 1961):140-4; 23(January-April 1962):166-8.*

CRITICAL AND BIOGRAPHICAL BOOKS

1 ATKINS, John. *George Orwell: A Literary and Biographical Study.* London: Calder, 1965.

2 BRANDER, L. *George Orwell.* London: Longmans, Green, 1954.

3 CALDER, Jenni. *Chronicles of Conscience: A Study of George Orwell and Arthur Koestler.* London: Secker and Warburg, 1968.†

4 HOLLIS, Christopher. *A Study of George Orwell: The Man and His Works.* London: Hollis and Carter, 1956.*

5 HOPKINSON, Tom. *George Orwell.* London: Longmans, Green, 1950. [British Council pamphlet.]

6 REES, Richard. *George Orwell: Fugitive from the Camp of Victory.* Carbondale, Ill.: Southern Illinois U P, 1961.*†

7 THOMAS, E. M. *George Orwell.* Edinburgh: Oliver and Boyd, 1965.

8 VOORHEES, Richard. *The Paradox of George Orwell.* Lafayette, Ind.: Purdue U, 1961. [Purdue U Studies. Humanities Series #1.]

9 WILLIAMS, Raymond. *George Orwell.* New York: Viking, 1971.†

10 WOODCOCK, George. *The Crystal Spirit: A Study of George Orwell.* Boston: Little, Brown, 1966.*†

CRITICAL ESSAYS

11 DEUTSCHER, Isaac. "1984–The Mysticism of Cruelty." *Heretics and Renegades.* London: Hamilton, 1955, pp. 35-50.

12 DOOLEY, D. J. "The Limitations of George Orwell." *UTQ* 28(1958-1959): 291-9.

13 DYSON, A. E. "Orwell: Irony as Prophecy." See 11.10, pp. 197-219.*

14 EDRICH, Emmanuel. "George Orwell and the Satire in Horror." *TSLL* 4 (1962):96-108.

15 FYVELL, T. R. "George Orwell and Eric Blair." *Encounter* 13(July 1959): 60-5.

16 HEPPENSTALL, Rayner. *Four Absentees.* London: Barrie and Rockliff, 1960, pp. 20-8, 58-64, 82-8, 139-46, 152-4, 157-9, 173-7, and *passim.*

17 HOGGART, Richard. "George Orwell and the Road to Wigan Pier." *CritQ* 7(Spring 1965):72-85.

18 HOWE, Irving. "Orwell: History as Nightmare." See 14.7, pp. 235-51.

19 KARL, Frederick R. "George Orwell: The White Man's Burden." See 16.5, pp. 148-66.

1 KING, Carlyle. "The Politics of George Orwell." *UTQ* 26(October 1956): 79-91.

2 LEWIS, Wyndham. "Orwell, or Two and Two Make Four." *The Writer and the Absolute.* London: Methuen, 1952, pp. 150-93.

3 MANDER, John. "One Step Forward: Two Steps Back." *The Writer and Commitment.* London: Secker and Warburg, 1961, pp. 71-110.

4 POTTS, Paul. "Don Quixote on a Bicycle." *Dante Called You Beatrice.* London: Eyre and Spottiswoode, 1960, pp. 71-87.

5 POWELL, Anthony. "George Orwell: A Memoir." *Atlantic Monthly* 220(October 1967):62-8.

6 QUINTANA, Ricardo. "George Orwell: The Satiric Resolution." *WSCL* 2,i(1961):31-8.*

7 RAHV, Philip. "The Unfuture of Utopia." *PR* 16(1949):743-9.*

8 RANALD, Ralph A. "George Orwell and the Mad World: The Anti-Universe of *1984.*" *SAQ* 66(1967):544-53.

9 SLATER, Joseph. "The Fictional Values of *1984.*" *Essays in Literary History: Presented to J. Milton French.* Ed. Rudolf Kirk and C. F. Main. New Brunswick: Rutgers U P, 1960, pp. 249-64.

10 STRACHEY, John. *The Strangled Cry.* London: Bodley Head, 1962, pp. 23-32.

11 SYMONS, Julian. "Orwell–A Reminiscence." *LonM* 3,vi(1963):35-49.

12 THALE, Jerome. "Orwell's Modest Proposal." *CritQ* 4(1962):365-8.

13 THOMPSON, Frank H., Jr. "Orwell's Image of the Man of Good Will." *CE* 22(1961):235-40.

14 TRILLING, Lionel. "George Orwell and the Politics of Truth." *Com* 13(March 1952):218-37. Repr. in Trilling, *The Opposing Self.* New York: Viking, 1955, pp. 151-72. [See also Introduction to 92.8.] *

15 WADSWORTH, Frank. "Orwell as Novelist: The Early Work." *UKCR* 22,ii(1955):93-9.

16 WAIN, John. "George Orwell (I)" and "George Orwell (II)." *Essays on Literature and Ideas.* London: Macmillan, 1963, pp. 180-93, 194-213.

17 WILLIAMS, Raymond. "George Orwell." See 50.13, pp. 304-13.*†

18 WOLLHEIM, Richard. "Orwell Reconsidered." *PR* 27(Winter 1960):82-97.

Anthony Powell (1905-)

TEXTS

19 *A Dance to the Music of Time: A Question of Upbringing, A Buyer's Market, The Acceptance World.* Boston: Little, Brown, 1955. London: Heinemann, 1962.†

1 *A Dance to the Music of Time, Second Movement: At Lady Molly's, Casanova's Chinese Restaurant, The Kindly Ones.* Boston: Little, Brown, 1964.

2 *Venusberg.* New ed. London: Heinemann, 1955.

3 *What's Become of Waring.* Harmondsworth, Middlesex: Penguin, 1962.

4 *Afternoon Men, a Novel.* Boston: Little, Brown, 1963. [1st American ed.]

5 *From a View to a Death.* Boston: Little, Brown, 1968. [1st American ed.]

6 *John Aubrey and His Friends.* London: Heinemann, 1963. [Critical study.]

7 WEATHERBY, W. J. "Taken from Life." *TC* 170(1961-1962):50-3. [Report on statements by Powell on his work.]

BIBLIOGRAPHIES

There is no separate bibliography.

CRITICAL AND BIOGRAPHICAL BOOKS

8 BERGONZI, Bernard. "Anthony Powell." In *Anthony Powell and L. P. Hartley*, by Paul Bloomfield and Bernard Bergonzi. London: Longmans, Green, 1962. [British Council pamphlet.]

9 MORRIS, Robert K. *The Novels of Anthony Powell.* Pittsburgh: U of Pittsburgh P, 1968.†

CRITICAL ESSAYS

10 AMIS, Kingsley. "Afternoon World." *Spectator* 194(May 13, 1955):619-20.

11 BOWEN, Elizabeth. "Three Novels by an English Writer with a Keen and Sardonic Eye." *NYHTB* 29(February 15, 1953):1,8.

12 BROOKE, Jocelyn. "From Wauchop to Widmerpool." *LonM* 7(September 1960):60-4.

13 DAVIS, Douglas M. "An Interview with Anthony Powell, Frome, England, June 1962." *CE* 24(1963):533-6.

14 "From a Chase to a View." *TLS* (February 16, 1951):100.

15 HALL, James. "The Uses of Polite Surprise, Anthony Powell." *EIC* 12(1962):167-83. Repr. in 16.2, pp. 129-50.

16 KARL, Frederick R. "Anthony Powell's *The Music of Time.*" See 16.5, pp. 238-44.

17 KERMODE, Frank. "The Interpretation of the Times (Christopher Isherwood and Anthony Powell)." *Encounter* 15(1960):74-6. Repr. in 16.6, pp. 126-30.

1 LECLAIRE, L. "Anthony Powell: Biographie spirituelle d'une génération." *EA* 9(1956):23-7.

2 MC CALL, Raymond. "Anthony Powell's Gallery." *CE* 27(1965):227-32.

3 MAYNE, Richard. "Incidental Music by Anthony Powell." *New Statesman and Nation* 64(July 6, 1962):17-8.

4 MIZENER, Arthur. "A Dance to the Music of Time: The Novels of Anthony Powell." *KR* 22(Winter 1960):79-92.*

5 PRITCHETT, V. S. "Books in General." *New Statesman and Nation* 43(June 28, 1952):307.*

6 PRITCHETT, V. S. "The Bored Barbarians." See 16.11, pp. 294-303.*

7 QUESENBERY, W. D. "Anthony Powell: The Anatomy of Decay." *Crit* 7,i(1964):5-26.

8 RADNER, Sanford. "Powell's Early Novels: A Study in Point of View." *Ren* 16(1964):194-200.

9 RUOFF, Gene W. "Social Mobility and the Artist in *Manhattan Transfer* and *The Music of Time.*" *WSCL* 5(1964):64-76.

10 RUSSELL, John. "Quintet from the 30's: Anthony Powell." *KR* 27(1965): 698-726.

11 SHAPIRO, Charles. "Widmerpool and *The Music of Time.*" See 16.16, pp. 81-94.

12 VINSON, James. "Anthony Powell's *Music of Time.*" *Per* 10(1958):146-52.

13 VOORHEES, Richard. "Anthony Powell: The First Phase." *PrS* 28(1954): 337-44.

14 WAUGH, Evelyn. "Marriage à la Mode–1936." *Spectator* 204(June 24, 1960):919.

15 WAUGH, Evelyn. "Bioscope." *Spectator* 206(June 29, 1962):863.

16 WEST, Anthony. "Wry Humor." *NY* 28(December 13, 1952):170-80.

John Cowper Powys (1872-1963)

TEXTS

There is no collected edition. Since 1951 Macdonald (London) has published new works by Powys and has reprinted earlier works, including novels. Many Macdonald editions have prefaces or introductions by Powys.

17 *A Glastonbury Romance.* Preface by Powys. New ed. London: Macdonald, 1955.*

18 *Wolf Solent.* London: Macdonald, 1961. [Also in Penguin Modern Classics, 1964.] *

19 *Maiden Castle.* Prefatory note by Malcolm Elwin. New ed. London: Macdonald, 1966.

1 POWYS, John Cowper, with Llewelyn POWYS. *Confessions of Two Brothers.* Rochester: Manas, 1916. [J. C. Powys, pp. 9-175.]

2 *Autobiography.* London: Macdonald, 1967.*

3 *Letters of John Cowper Powys to Louis Wilkinson 1935-1956.* London: Macdonald, 1958.

BIBLIOGRAPHIES

4 LANGRIDGE, Derek W. *John Cowper Powys: A Record of Achievement.* London: Library Association, 1966.*

CRITICAL AND BIOGRAPHICAL BOOKS

5 CHURCHILL, R. C. *The Powys Brothers.* London: Longmans, Green, 1962. [British Council pamphlet. Includes selected bibliography.]

6 COLLINS, H. P. *John Cowper Powys: Old Earth Man.* London: Barrie and Rockliff, 1966.

7 HOPKINS, Kenneth. *The Powys Brothers: A Biographical Appreciation.* London: Phoenix House, 1967, especially pp. 132-8, 220-54, and *passim.**

8 KNIGHT, G. Wilson. *The Saturnian Quest: A Chart of the Prose Works of John Cowper Powys.* London: Methuen, 1964.*

9 "MARLOW, Louis" (Louis Wilkinson). "John Cowper." *Welsh Ambassadors.* London: Chapman and Hall, 1936, pp. 114-60.

10 WARD, Richard Heron. "John Cowper Powys." *The Powys Brothers.* London: Bodley Head, 1935, pp. 1-80.

CRITICAL ESSAYS
The first title is a collection.

11 *REL* 4,i(January 1963). Number in honor of John Cowper Powys.

12 AURY, Dominique. "Reading Powys." *REL* 4,i(1963):33-7.

13 "Bookworm Turned Fabulist." *TLS* (August 12, 1955):460.

14 CHANING-PEARCE, Melville. *The Terrible Crystal: Studies in Kierkegaard and Modern Christianity.* New York: Oxford U P, 1941, pp. 179-93. [On D. H. Lawrence and Powys.]

15 "Cosmic Correspondences." *TLS* (October 11, 1957):601-2.

16 DAVIES, Frederick. "John Cowper Powys et le Roi Lear." *LetN* (July-August-September 1965):108-15.

17 ELWIN, Malcolm. "John Cowper Powys." In 91.13, Baker, pp. 117-34.

18 GRESSET, Michel. "John Cowper Powys Notre Contemporain." *Preuves* 163(Spring 1964):74-8.

19 GRESSET, Michel. "Les Rites Matinaux de John Cowper Powys." *CS* 53rd année, no. 386(1966):85-9.

20 HANLEY, James. "The Man in the Corner." *John O'London's Weekly* (September 3, 1954):877-8.

21 HENTSCHEL, Cedric. "John Cowper Powys and the 'Gretchen-Cult.' " *SN* 15(1942): 91-104.*

22 KNIGHT, G. Wilson. "Lawrence, Joyce, and Powys." *EIC* 11(1961):403-17.

23 KNIGHT, G. Wilson. "Owen Glendower." *REL* 4,i(1963):41-52.

1 MILLER, Henry. *The Books in My Life.* London: Owen, 1952, pp. 32, 126, 134-9, 146, 170, 199, 210, 248-50, 251-2.

2 PRITCHETT, V. S. "The Mysteries of John Cowper Powys." *New Statesman* 69(April 2, 1965):534-5.

3 REDA, Jacques. "L'insaisissable: Notes sur l'autobiographie de J. C. Powys." *CS* 53,No. 386(1966):77-84.

4 REID, Margaret J. C. *The Arthurian Legend.* Edinburgh: Oliver and Boyd, 1938, pp. 150, 154-7. (On *A Glastonbury Romance.*]

5 WAHL, Jean. "Un defenseur de la vie sensuelle." *Poésie, pensée, perception.* Paris: Calmann-Levy, 1948, pp. 190-216.

6 WAHL, Jean. "J. C. Powys." *LetN* 60(May 1958):650-5.

7 WILKINSON, Louis. "The Brothers Powys." *Essays by Divers Hands*, Vol. XXIV. Ed. Clifford Bax. London: Oxford U P, 1948.

8 WILSON, Angus. "Mythology in John Cowper Powys's Novels." *REL* 4,i(1963):9-20.*

9 WILSON, Colin. "The Swamp and the Desert: Notes on Powys and Hemingway." See 90.14, pp. 113-21.

T. (Theodore) F. (Francis) Powys (1875-1953)

TEXTS

10 *Mr. Weston's Good Wine.* London: Chatto and Windus, 1941 (Crown Octavo Edition), 1960, 1964.

11 *Mr. Weston's Good Wine.* Introduction by David Holbrook. London: Heinemann, 1967. [Heinemann Educational Books.]

12 *Rosie Plum and Other Stories.* Foreword by Francis Powys. London: Chatto and Windus, 1966.

13 *Two Stories: "Come and Dine" and "Tadnol."* Ed. Peter Riley. Hastings, Sussex, Brimmell, 1967.

14 "Why I Have Given up Writing." *John O'London's Weekly and Outlook* 36(October 23, 1936):145-6, 152. [Interview.]

BIBLIOGRAPHIES

15 RILEY, Peter. *A Bibliography of T. F. Powys.* Hastings, Sussex: Brimmell, 1967. [Also contains bibliography of works on T. F. Powys.] *

CRITICAL AND BIOGRAPHICAL BOOKS

16 COOMBES, H. *T. F. Powys.* London: Barrie and Rockliff, 1960.*

1 HUNTER, William. *The Novels and Stories of T. F. Powys.* Cambridge: Frazer, 1931. [Minority Pamphlet No. 3.]

CRITICAL ESSAYS
The first title is a collection. Individual essays follow.

2 SEWELL, Brocard, ed. *Theodore: Essays on T. F. Powys by Neville Braybrooke (and Others) with a Story by T. F. Powys, "The Useless Woman," and Some Letters of T. F. Powys to Littleton C. Powys and Elizabeth Myers.* Aylesford, Kent: St. Albert's, 1964.

3 BRAYBROOKE, Neville. "Mr. Weston's Good Vintage." See 99.2, pp. 48-54.

4 CARR, W. I. "Reflections on T. F. Powys." *English* 15(Spring 1964):8-12.*

5 CHURCHILL, R. C. "The Path of T. F. Powys." *The Critic* 1(Spring 1947): 25-31.

6 CHURCHILL, R. C. See 97.5, pp. 18-31.

7 HOLBROOK, David. "T. F. Powys and Dylan Thomas." See 8.3, Ford, pp. 415-28.

8 HOPKINS, Kenneth. See 97.7, pp. 77-83, 124-31.

9 KERMODE, Frank. "The Art of T. F. Powys, Ironist." *Welsh Review* (Cardiff) 6,iii(1947):205-19.*

10 LAS VERGNAS, Raymond. "L'homme tranquil du Dorset: Theodore Francis Powys." *RdP* 72(September 1965):98-103.*

11 MAC CAMPBELL, D. "The Art of T. F. Powys." *SR* 42(1934):461-73.

12 "MARLOW, Louis" (Louis Wilkinson). "Theodore (1908-1935)." See 97.9, pp. 161-210.

13 RILEY, A. P. "The Original Ending of *Mr. Weston's Good Wine.*" *REL* 8,ii(1967):49-55.

14 STEINMANN, Martin, Jr. "The Symbolism of T. F. Powys." *Crit* 1,ii(1957): 49-63.*

15 STEINMANN, Martin, Jr. "Water and Animal Symbolism in T. F. Powys." *ES* 41(1960):359-65.

16 VAN KRANENDONK, A. G. "Theodore Powys." *English Studies* (Amsterdam) 26(1944-1945):97-107.

17 WARD, Richard Heron. "T. F. Powys." See 97.10, pp. 83-143.

18 WARREN, C. "The Novels of T. F. Powys." *The Criterion* 7,iv(1928):134-7.

19 WILSON, Joy. "T. F. Powys 'The Moods of God.' " See 99.2, Sewell, pp. 32-40.

Dorothy (Miller) Richardson (1873-1957)

TEXTS

1 *Pilgrimage.* With a new introduction by Walter Allen. 4 vols. I: *Pointed Roofs, Backwater, Honeycomb.* II: *The Tunnel, Interim.* III: *Deadlock, Revolving Lights, The Trap.* IV: *Oberland, Dawn's Left Hand, Clear Horizon, Dimple Hill, March Moonlight.* London: Dent, 1967. [This edition contains an additional section, *March Moonlight*, not previously published.]

2 *Pilgrimage.* 4 vols. New York: Knopf, 1938, 1967.

3 "Beginnings: A Brief Sketch." See 91.4, pp. 195-8. [See also bibliography, pp. 199-207.]

4 "Journey to Paradise." *Fortnightly Review* 129(1928):407-14. [Childhood recollections.]

5 "Data for Spanish Publisher." Ed. Joseph Prescott. *LonM* 6(June, 1959): 14-9. [Autobiographical.]

BIBLIOGRAPHIES

6 GLIKIN, Gloria. "A Checklist of Writings by Dorothy M. Richardson." *ELT* 8,i(1965):1-11.*

7 GLIKIN, Gloria. "Dorothy M. Richardson: An Annotated Bibliography of Writings About Her." *ELT* 8,i(1965):12-35.*

8 PRESCOTT, Joseph. "A Preliminary Checklist of Periodical Publications of Dorothy M. Richardson." See 46.14, Wallace and Ross, pp. 219-25.*

CRITICAL AND BIOGRAPHICAL BOOKS

9 BLAKE, Caesar R. *Dorothy Richardson.* Ann Arbor: U of Michigan P, 1960.

10 GREGORY, Horace. *Dorothy Richardson: An Adventure in Self-Discovery.* New York: Holt, Rinehart and Winston, 1967.

11 POWYS, John Cowper. *Dorothy M. Richardson.* London: Joiner and Steele, 1931.

CRITICAL ESSAYS

12 BEACH, Joseph Warren. "Imagism: Dorothy Richardson." See 11.1, pp. 385-400.*

13 BERESFORD, J. D. "Experiment in the Novel." *Tradition and Experiment in Present-Day Literature.* London: Oxford U P, 1929, pp. 23-53.

14 "Dorothy Richardson: 1919." *TLS* (August 28, 1953):xii.

1 DREW, Elizabeth. See 7.18, pp. 84-8 and *passim.*

2 EAGLESON, Harvey. "Pedestal for Statue: The Novels of Dorothy M. Richardson." *SR* 42(1934):42-53.

3 EDEL, Leon. See 13.13, pp. 46-9, 101-11, and *passim.* *

4 GLIKIN, Gloria. "Dorothy M. Richardson: The Personal 'Pilgrimage.' " *PMLA* 78(1963):586-600. [Biographical study.] *

5 GLIKIN, Gloria. "Variations on a Method." *James Joyce Quarterly* 2,i(1964):42-9.

6 GREENE, Graham. "The Saratoga Trunk." See 54.8, pp. 149-52.

7 HOOPS, Reinald. See 5.2, pp. 151-4.

8 HUMPHREY, Robert. See 12.1, pp. 9-12, 34-5, 78-80.

9 HYDE, Lawrence. "The Work of Dorothy Richardson." *The Adelphi* 2(1924):508-17.

10 KELLY, Robert G. "The Strange Philosophy of Dorothy M. Richardson." *Pacific Spectator* 8(1954):76-82.

11 KUMAR, Shiv K. "Dorothy Richardson and the Dilemma of 'Being Versus Becoming.' " *MLN* 74(1959):494-501.

12 MEYERHOFF, Hans. See 12.12, pp. 11-26.

13 MURRY, John Middleton. "The Break-up of the Novel." *YR* 12(1922): 288-304.

14 MYERS, Walter L. *The Later Realism*, pp. 73-8, 84-5, 119-22, 135-7, 149-53, 158-9, and *passim.* *

15 PRIESTLEY, J. B. "Proust, Joyce, and Miss Richardson." *Spectator* 130(1923):1084-5.

16 ROURKE, Constance. "Dorothy M. Richardson." *New Republic* 20(November 26, 1919):pt. 2, p.14.

17 SINCLAIR, May. "The Novels of Dorothy Richardson." *The Egoist* 5(April 1918):57-9.*

18 TRICKETT, Rachel. "The Living Dead–V: Dorothy Richardson." *LonM* 6(June 1959):20-5.

C. (Charles) P. (Percy) Snow (1905-)

TEXTS

19 Uniform Edition. London: Macmillan. New York: Scribner's [Includes novels in the "Strangers and Brothers" sequence. Several of the "Strangers and Brothers" novels have also appeared as English and American paperbacks, among these *The Masters*, *The Conscience of the Rich*, *The New Men*, and *Time of Hope.*]

1 *The Two Cultures and the Scientific Revolution.* Cambridge and New York: Cambridge U P, 1959.

2 *Variety of Men.* London: Macmillan, 1967. [Essays and reminiscences.]

BIBLIOGRAPHIES

3 RABINOVITZ, Rubin. "Bibliography." See 8.21, pp. 196-211.*

4 STONE, Bernard. "Bibliography." See 102.7, Greacen, pp. 41-64.

CRITICAL AND BIOGRAPHICAL BOOKS

5 COOPER, William. *C. P. Snow.* London: Longmans, Green, 1959. [British Council pamphlet.]

6 DAVIS, Robert Gorham. *C. P. Snow.* New York: Columbia U P, 1965. [Columbia Essays on Modern Writers.]

7 GREACEN, Robert. *The World of C. P. Snow.* New York: London House and Maxwell, 1963.*

8 KARL, Frederick. *The Politics of Conscience: The Novels of C. P. Snow.* Carbondale, Ill.: Southern Illinois U P, 1963.†

9 LEAVIS, F. R. *The Two Cultures: The Significance of C. P. Snow.* New York: Random House, 1963. [Contains new preface and an essay on Snow's Reade Lecture by Michael Yudkin.]

10 THALE, Jerome. *C. P. Snow.* Edinburgh: Oliver and Boyd, 1964. [Includes bibliography, pp. 108-12.] *

CRITICAL ESSAYS
The first title is a collection.

11 CORNELIUS, David K., and Edwin ST. VINCENT, eds. *Cultures in Conflict: Perspectives on the Snow-Leavis Controversy.* Chicago: Scott, Foresman, 1964.

12 ALLEN, Walter. "*The Masters*: C. P. Snow." *Reading a Novel.* London: Phoenix House, 1963, pp. 46-50.

13 BERGONZI, Bernard. "The World of Lewis Eliot." *TC* 167(1960):214-25.*

14 GARDNER, Helen. "The World of C. P. Snow." *New Statesman* 55(1958): 409-10.*

15 HALL, William F. "The Humanism of C. P. Snow." *WSCL* 4(1963):199-208.

16 HAMILTON, Kenneth. "C. P. Snow and Political Man." *QQ* 69(1962): 416-27.*

17 HEPPENSTALL, Rayner. *The Fourfold Tradition: Notes on the French and English Literatures with Some Ethnological and Historical Asides.* New York: New Directions, 1961, pp. 224-43.

1 JOHNSON, Pamela Hansford. "Three Novelists and the Drawing of Character." *E&S* 3(1950):81-91.

2 KAZIN, Alfred. "A Gifted Boy from the Midlands." *Reporter* 20(February 5, 1959):37-9.*

3 KERMODE, Frank. "The House of Fiction: Interviews with Seven English Novelists." *PR* 30(Spring 1963):61-82.

4 MANDEL, E. W. "C. P. Snow's Fantasy of Politics." *QQ* 69(1962):24-37.*

5 MARTIN, Graham. "C. P. Snow." See 8.3, Ford, pp. 409-14.

6 MILLGATE, Michael. "Structure and Style in the Novels of C. P. Snow." *REL* 1(April 1960):34-41.*

7 NOTT, Kathleen. "The Type to Which the Whole Creation Moves?" *Encounter* 18(February 1962):87-8, 94-7.

8 RABINOVITZ, Rubin. See 8.21. "C. P. Snow as Literary Critic," pp. 97-127. "C. P. Snow as Novelist," pp. 128-71.*

9 STANFORD, Derek. "C. P. Snow: The Novelist as Fox." *Meanjin* 19(1960): 236-51.*

10 STANFORD, Raney. "Personal Politics in the Novels of C. P. Snow." *Crit* 2(Spring-Summer 1958):16-28.

11 STANFORD, Raney. "The Achievement of C. P. Snow." *WHR* 16(1962): 43-52.

12 TRILLING, Lionel. "The Novel Alive or Dead." *A Gathering of Fugitives.* Boston: Beacon, 1956, pp. 125-32.

13 TRILLING, Lionel. "Science, Literature and Culture, a Comment on the Leavis-Snow Controversy." *Com* 33(1962):461-77.*

J. (John) R. (Ronald) R. (Reuel) Tolkien (1892-)

TEXTS

14 *The Hobbit: or There and Back Again.* Illus. by the author. Boston: Houghton Mifflin, 1938. London: Allen and Unwin, 1958.

15 *The Lord of the Rings.* 3 vols. (*The Fellowship of the Ring. The Two Towers. The Return of the King.*) London: Allen and Unwin, 1954-1955. 2d ed. 1966. Boston: Houghton Mifflin, 1963. 2d ed., 1965-1966, rev. ed., 1967. New York: Ballantine Books, 1969. Newly rev. with foreword by the author.†

16 "On Fairy Stories." In *Essays Presented to Charles Williams*, ed. C. S. Lewis. London: Oxford U P, 1947, pp. 38-89. Grand Rapids, Mich.: Eerdmans, 1966. [Essay reprinted in *Tree and Leaf.* London: Allen and Unwin, 1964. Boston: Houghton Mifflin, 1965. Also in *The Tolkien Reader.* Boston, Houghton Mifflin, 1966. New York: Ballantine, 1967.] †

1 "*Beowulf:* The Monsters and the Critics." *PBA* 22(1936):245-95. Repr. London: Oxford U P, 1958.

BIBLIOGRAPHIES

2 WEST, Richard C. "An Annotated Bibliography of Tolkien Criticism." *Extrapolation* 10(1968):17-45. [Covers period from 1920s to mid-1968. Entries inclusive rather than selective.]

CRITICAL AND BIOGRAPHICAL BOOKS
There are no substantive critical books.

CRITICAL ESSAYS
The first title is a collection.

3 ISAACS, Neil D., and Rose A. Zimbardo, eds. *Tolkien and the Critics: Essays on J.R.R. Tolkien's* The Lord of the Rings. Notre Dame and London: U of Notre Dame P, 1968. [Includes 15 critical essays.] *†

4 AUDEN, W. H. "The Quest Hero." *TQ* 4(1961):81-93. Repr. in 104.3*

5 AUDEN, W. H. "Good and Evil in *The Lord of the Rings." CritQ* 10(1968): 138-42.

6 COX, C. B. "The World of the Hobbits." *Spectator* 217(1966):844.

7 LEARD, F. "L'épopée religieuse de J. R. R. Tolkien." *EA* 20(1967):265-81.

8 PARKER, Douglass. "Hwaet, We Holbytla." *HudR* 9(1956-1957):598-609.

9 ROBERTS, Mark. "Adventure in English." *EIC* 6(1956):450-9.

10 RYAN, J. S. "German Mythology Applied–The Extension of the Literary Folk Memory." *Folklore* 77(1966):45-59.

11 THOMSON, George H. "*The Lord of the Rings:* The Novel as Traditional Romance." *WSCL* 8(1967):43-59.

12 WILSON, Edmund. "Oo, Those Awful Orcs!" *The Nation* 182,xv(1956): 312-4. Repr. in Wilson, *The Bit Between My Teeth: A Literary Chronicle of 1950-1965.* New York: Farrar, Straus and Giroux, 1965, pp. 326-32.

13 WOJCIK, Jan, S.J. "Tolkien and Coleridge: Remaking of the 'Green Earth.'" *Ren* 20(1968):134-9, 146.

Rex Warner (1905-)

TEXTS

14 *The Aerodrome: A Love Story.* London: Bodley Head; Boston: Little, Brown, 1966.†

1 *The Young Caesar.* New York: New American Library, Mentor, 1958.†

2 *Imperial Caesar.* Boston: Little, Brown, 1960.

3 *Pericles the Athenian.* Boston: Little, Brown, 1963.

4 *The Cult of Power: Essays.* Philadelphia: Lippincott, 1947.

BIBLIOGRAPHIES

5 MC LEOD, A. L. "A Rex Warner Bibliography." See 105.7, pp. 87-98.

CRITICAL AND BIOGRAPHICAL BOOK

6 MC LEOD, A. L. *Rex Warner: Writer.* Sydney: Wentworth, 1960.

CRITICAL ESSAYS
The first two titles are collections.

7 MC LEOD, A. L., ed. *The Achievement of Rex Warner.* Sydney: Wentworth, 1965.

8 RAJAN, B., and Andrew PEARSE, eds. *Focus One: Kafka and Rex Warner.* London: Dobson, 1945.*

9 DAY LEWIS, C. *The Buried Day.* London: Chatto and Windus, pp. 161-3 and *passim.* [Reminiscences of Warner at Oxford.]

10 DE VITIS, A. A. "Rex Warner and the Cult of Power." *TCL* 6(1960): 107-16. Repr. in 105.7.

11 DRENNER, Don V. R. "Kafka, Warner, and the Cult of Power." *KM* (1952):62-4.

12 GORLIER, Claudio. "Rex Warner." *Paragone* 2(April 1951):76-80. [In Italian.]

13 KARL, Frederick R. "The Novel as Moral Allegory." See 16.5, pp. 265-9.

14 MAINI, Darshan Singh. "Rex Warner's Political Novels: An Allegorical Crusade Against Fascism." *IJES* 2(1961):91-107. Repr. in 105.7.

1 NEWBY, P. H. See 8.18, pp. 23-4.

2 PRITCHETT, V. S. "Rex Warner." See 53.3, Baker, pp. 304-9. Repr. in 105.7.*

3 RAJAN, B. "Kafka—A Comparison with Rex Warner." See 105.8, pp. 1-14.*

4 STRAUSS, Harold. "To New Horizons in the Novel." *NYTBR* (January 23, 1938):2.

5 WOODCOCK, George. "Kafka and Rex Warner." See 15.15, pp. 197-206.

Evelyn Waugh (1903-1966)

TEXTS

6 *The Novels of Evelyn Waugh.* Uniform Edition. London: Chapman and Hall. [Many of Waugh's novels are presently in print in both English and American paperbacks.]

7 *Men at Arms. Officers and Gentlemen. Unconditioned Surrender.* London: Penguin, 1964.

8 ROLO, Charles J., ed. *The World of Evelyn Waugh.* Boston: Little, Brown, 1958. [Selection of Waugh's writing with introduction by Rolo.]

9 *A Little Learning: The First Volume of an Autobiography.* London: Chapman and Hall, 1964.*

BIBLIOGRAPHIES

10 DOYLE, P. A. "Evelyn Waugh: A Bibliography (1926-1956)." *BB* 22(May-August 1957): 57-62.*

11 KOSOK, Heinz. "Evelyn Waugh: A Checklist of Criticism." *TCL* 11(1965): 211-5.*

12 LINCK, Charles E., Jr. "Works of Evelyn Waugh, 1910-1930." *TCL* 10(1964):19-25.

CRITICAL AND BIOGRAPHICAL BOOKS

13 BRADBURY, Malcolm. *Evelyn Waugh.* Edinburgh: Oliver and Boyd, 1964.

14 CARENS, James F. *The Satiric Art of Evelyn Waugh.* Seattle: U of Washington P, 1966.*†

15 DE VITIS, A. A. *Roman Holiday: The Catholic Novels of Evelyn Waugh.* New York: Bookman, 1956.*

16 DONALDSON, Frances. *Evelyn Waugh: Portrait of a Country Neighbour.* London: Weidenfeld and Nicolson, 1967.

1 HOLLIS, Christopher. *Evelyn Waugh.* London: Longmans, Green, 1954. [British Council pamphlet.]

2 STOPP, Frederick J. *Evelyn Waugh: Portrait of an Artist.* London: Chapman and Hall, 1958.*

CRITICAL ESSAYS

3 ACTON, H. *Memoirs of an Aesthete.* London: Methuen, 1948, *passim.*

4 BENEDICT, Stewart H. "The Candide Figure in the Novels of Evelyn Waugh." *PMASAL* 48(1963):685-9.

5 BERGONZI, Bernard. "Evelyn Waugh's Gentlemen." *CritQ* 5(Spring 1963): 23-36.

6 BLUMENBERG, Hans. "Eschatologische Ironie: Uber die Romane Evelyn Waughs." *Hochland* 46(1953-1954):241-51.*

7 DAVIS, Robert Murray. "Evelyn Waugh on the Art of Fiction." *PELL*, 2(1966):243-52.

8 DENNIS, Nigel. "Evelyn Waugh and the Churchillian Renaissance." *PR* 10(1943):350-61.

9 DYSON, A. E. "Evelyn Waugh and the Mysteriously Disappearing Hero." *CritQ* 2(Spring 1960):72-9. Repr. in 11.10, pp. 187-96.*

10 FIELDING, Gabriel. "Evelyn Waugh and the Cross of Satire." *The Critic* 23(February-March 1965):52-6.

11 GREEN, Peter. "Du Côte de Chez Waugh." *REL* 2(April 1961):89-100.

12 GREENE, George. "Scapegoat with Style: The Status of Evelyn Waugh." *QQ* 71(1965):485-93.

13 HALL, James. "Stylized Rebellion: Evelyn Waugh." See 16.2, pp. 45-65.

14 HARDY, John Edward. "*Brideshead Revisited*: God, Man, and Others." See 16.3, pp. 159-74.

15 HINCHCLIFFE, Peter. "Fathers and Children in the Novels of Evelyn Waugh." *UTQ* 35(1966):293-310.*

16 HINES, Leo. "Waugh and His Critics." *Cweal* 76,iii(1962):60-3.

17 JEBB, Julian. "Evelyn Waugh: An Interview." *ParR* 8(Summer-Fall 1963): 73-85.

18 KARL, Frederick R. "The World of Evelyn Waugh: The Morally Insane." See 16.5, pp. 167-82.

19 KERMODE, Frank. "Mr. Waugh's Cities." See 16.6, pp. 164-75.*

20 KERNAN, Alvin. "The Wall and the Jungle: The Early Novels of Evelyn Waugh." *YR* 53(1963):199-220.*

21 LA FRANCE, Marston. "Context and Structure of Evelyn Waugh's *Brideshead Revisited.*" *TCL* 10(1964):12-18.

22 LAPICQUE, F. "La satire dans l'oeuvre d'Evelyn Waugh." *EA* 10(July-September 1957):193-215.

1 LINKLATER, Eric. "Evelyn Waugh." *The Art of Adventure.* London: Macmillan, 1948, pp. 44-58.

2 MACAULAY, Rose. "The Best and the Worst, II. Evelyn Waugh." *Horizon* 14(December 1946):360-76. Repr. in 91.13, Baker, pp. 135-51.

3 MARCUS, Stephen. "Evelyn Waugh and the Art of Entertainment." *PR* 23(1956):348-57.

4 MENEN, A. "The Baroque and Mr. Waugh." *Month* 5(1951):226-37.*

5 NICHOLS, James W. "Romantic and Realistic: The Tone of Evelyn Waugh's Early Novels." *CE* 24(1962):46, 51-6.

6 O'DONNELL, D. "The Pieties of Evelyn Waugh." See 15.2, pp. 109-23.

7 O'FAOLAIN, Sean. "Huxley and Waugh." See 15.3, pp. 31-69.

8 PRITCHETT, V. S. "Books in General." *New Statesman and Nation* 37(1949):473-4.*

9 RAVEN, Simon. "Waugh's Private Wars." *Spectator* 212(1964):798.

10 SAVAGE, D. S. "The Innocence of Evelyn Waugh." See 16.12, Rajan, pp. 34-46.

11 SPENDER, Stephen. "The World of Evelyn Waugh." See 9.2, pp. 159-74.*

12 WASSON, Richard. "A Handful of Dust: Critique of Victorianism." *MFS* 7(1961):327-37.

13 WAUGH, Alec. "My Brother Evelyn." *My Brother Evelyn and Other Portraits.* New York: Farrar, Straus and Giroux, 1967, pp. 162-98

14 WILSON, Colin. "Evelyn Waugh and Graham Greene." *The Strength to Dream: Literature and the Imagination.* Boston: Houghton Mifflin, 1962, pp. 42-55.

15 WILSON, Edmund. "Splendours and Miseries of Evelyn Waugh." See 6.14, pp. 298-305.*

H. (Herbert) G. (George) Wells (1866-1946)

TEXTS

16 *The Works of H. G. Wells.* Atlantic Edition. 28 vols. London: Unwin; New York: Scribner's, 1924-1927. [Although this edition is limited and incomplete, it was read and revised throughout by Wells, who wrote a preface for each volume and a general introduction to the edition as a whole.]

17 *Seven Famous Novels by H. G. Wells.* Preface by Wells. *The Time Machine. The Island of Dr. Moreau. The Invisible Man. The War of the Worlds. The First Men in the Moon. The Food of the Gods. In the Days of the Comet.* New York, Knopf, 1934. [Since published as *Seven Science Fiction Novels of H. G. Wells.* New York: Dover, 1950.]

1 *The Complete Short Stories of H. G. Wells.* London: Benn, 1966.

2 *The Last Books of H. G. Wells:* The Happy Turning *and* Mind at the End of its Tether. Ed. with introduction and appendix by G. P. Wells. London: H. G. Wells Society, 1968. [Introduction bears importantly on Wells's late work.]

3 *H. G. Wells: Journalism and Prophecy 1893-1946: An Anthology.* Comp. and ed. W. Warren Wagar. Boston: Houghton Mifflin, 1964. London: Bodley Head, 1965. [Includes essays and literary portraits.]

4 *Tono-Bungay.* Ed. Bernard Bergonzi. Boston: Houghton Mifflin, 1966. [This novel also published, New York: Modern Library, 1935; London: Longmans, Green, 1961, introduction and notes by A. C. Ward; New York: Signet Classics, 1961, foreword by Harry T. Moore.] †

5 *The Wheels of Chance and The Time Machine.* Introductory note by A. J. Hoppe. London: Dent; New York: Dutton, 1935. [915 Everyman's Library, 1961.]

6 *The History of Mr. Polly.* Ed. Gordon N. Ray. Boston: Houghton Mifflin, 1960.†

7 *A Modern Utopia.* Introduction by Mark Hillegas. Lincoln, Neb.: U of Nebraska P, 1967.

8 *The Invisible Man.* Introduction by Frank Wells. London: Collins, 1965. [Includes bibliography.]

9 *Experiment in Autobiography.* 2 vols. London: Gollancz, 1934; 1 vol. New York: Macmillan, 1934.

10 EDEL, Leon, and Gordon N. RAY, eds. *Henry James and H. G. Wells: A Record of Their Friendship, Their Debate on the Art of Fiction, and Their Quarrel.* Urbana, Ill.: U of Illinois P; London: Hart-Davis, 1958. [Extended introduction, pp. 15-41.] *

11 WILSON, Harris, ed. *Arnold Bennett and H. G. Wells.* See 17.10.

12 GETTMANN, Royal, ed. *George Gissing and H. G. Wells.* See 48.6.

BIBLIOGRAPHIES

13 RAY, Gordon N. "H. G. Wells's Contributions to the *Saturday Review.*" *Library* 16(March 1961):29-36.

14 THIRSK, James W. *H. G. Wells 1866-1946: A Centenary Book List.* London: Borough of Ealing Public Libraries, 1966. [Contains a record of all Wells's books except minor items.]

15 WELLS, Geoffrey H. *The Works of H. G. Wells 1887-1925: A Bibliography, Dictionary and Subject-Index.* London: Routledge, 1926. [Best bibliography on the years it covers.] *

16 *H. G. Wells: A Comprehensive Bibliography.* Comp. the H. G. Wells Society with a foreword by Kingsley Martin. London: H. G. Wells Society, 1966. [Wells items are annotated.] *

CRITICAL AND BIOGRAPHICAL BOOKS

1 BELGION, Montgomery. *H. G. Wells.* London: Longmans, Green, 1953. [British Council pamphlet.] *

2 BERGONZI, Bernard. *The Early H. G. Wells: A Study of the Scientific Romances.* Toronto: U of Toronto P, 1961.*

3 HILLEGAS, Mark. *The Future as Nightmare: H. G. Wells and the Anti-utopians.* New York: Oxford U P, 1967.

4 KAGARLITSKI, J. *The Life and Thought of H. G. Wells.* Trans. Moura Budberg. London: Sidgwick and Jackson, 1966. [A Soviet study.]

5 NICHOLSON, Norman. *H. G. Wells.* Denver: Swallow, 1950.*

6 RAKNEM, Ingvald. *H. G. Wells and His Critics.* New York: Hillary House, 1963. [Contains detailed bibliography, pp. 430-72.]

7 WAGAR, W. Warren. *H. G. Wells and the World State.* New Haven: Yale U P, 1961. (Useful bibliography, pp. 277-91.)*

8 "WEST, Geoffrey" (pseud. of Geoffrey H. Wells). *H. G. Wells: A Sketch for a Portrait.* Introduction by H. G. Wells. New York: Norton, 1930. [Good biographical material though not definitive.]

CRITICAL ESSAYS
The first title is a collection.

9 *The Wellsian.* Annual journal of scholarly articles on Wells published by the H. G. Wells Society since its founding in London, 1960.*

10 BECKER, Carl L. "Mr. Wells and the New History." *Everyman His Own Historian.* New York: Crofts, 1935, pp. 169-90.

11 BROWN, E. K. "Two Formulas for Fiction: Henry James and H. G. Wells." *CE* 8(1946):7-17.*

12 CAUDWELL, Christopher. "H. G. Wells: A Study in Utopianism." See 75.12, pp. 73-95.

13 EDGAR, Pelham. "H. G. Wells and the Modern Novel." See 11.11, pp. 217-28.

14 ELLIS, Havelock. "H. G. Wells." *From Marlowe to Shaw: The Studies, 1876-1936, in English Literature.* London: Williams and Norgate, 1950, pp. 297-302.

15 FRIERSON, W. C. See 8.6, pp. 183-8, 205-7.

16 GERBER, Richard. See 13.15, p. 13 and *passim.**

17 HILLEGAS, Mark. "The First Invasion from Mars." *Michigan Alumnus Quarterly Review* 66(Winter 1960):107-12.*

18 HUGHES, David Y. "H. G. Wells: Ironic Romancer." *Extrapolation* 6,ii(1965):32-8.*

1 KETTLE, Arnold. "H. G. Wells: *Tono-Bungay.*" See 16.7, II, pp. 89-95.

2 KEYNES, John Maynard. "Clissold." *Essays in Persuasion.* New York: Norton, 1963, pp. 349-57. [Review of *The World of William Clissold.*]

3 KRUTCH, Joseph Wood. "The Loss of Confidence." *ASch* 22(1952): 141-53.*

4 LAWRENCE, D. H. "Review of *The World of William Clissold* by H. G. Wells." See 72.9, pp. 133-8.

5 LODGE, David. "*Tono-Bungay* and the Condition of England." See 12.7, pp. 214-42.*

6 MAUROIS, André. "H. G. Wells." See 62.13, pp. 59-93.

7 MENCKEN, H. L. "The Late Mr. Wells." *Prejudices, First Series.* New York: Knopf, 1919, pp. 22-35.

8 NICKERSON, C. C. "A Note on Some Neglected Opinions of H. G. Wells." *EFT* 5,v(1962):27-30.

9 ORWELL, George. "Wells, Hitler and the World State." *Horizon* 4(August 1941):133-9. Repr. in 92.11, II, pp. 139-45.*

10 POSTON, Lawrence. "*Tono-Bungay:* Wells's Unconstructed Tale." *CE* 26(1965):433-8.*

11 PRITCHETT, V. S. "The Scientific Romances." See 16.11, pp. 160-9.*

12 RAY, Gordon N. "H. G. Wells Tries to Be a Novelist." *Edwardians and Late Victorians.* New York: Columbia U P, 1960. [English Institute Essays 1959.]

13 SEGUY, René. "H. G. Wells et la pensée contemporaine." *MdF* 95(1912): 673-99.*

14 SNOW, C. P. "H. G. Wells." See 102.2, pp. 47-64.

15 WEEKS, Robert P. "Disentanglement as a Theme in H. G. Wells's Fiction." *PMASAL* 39(1954):439-44.

16 WEST, Anthony. "H. G. Wells." *Encounter* 8(1957):52-9.*

Charles Williams (1886-1945)

TEXTS

Novels by Williams other than the following are published by Eerdmans, Grand Rapids, Mich.

17 *All Hallows' Eve.* Introduction by T. S. Eliot. New York: Noonday, 1966.†

18 *The Greater Trumps.* Preface by William Lindsay Gresham. New York: Noonday, 1966.†

1 *Collected Plays by Charles Williams.* Ed. John Heath-Stubbs. London: Oxford U P, 1963.

2 *The Image of the City: And Other Essays.* Ed. and with introduction by Anne Ridler. London: Oxford U P, 1958. [This introduction is one of the best to Williams and his work.] *

3 *Charles Williams: Selected Writings.* Ed. Anne Ridler. London: Oxford U P, 1961. [Represents Williams in all forms except fiction.]

BIBLIOGRAPHIES

4 DAWSON, Lawrence R., Jr. "A Checklist of Reviews by Charles Williams." *PBSA* 55(1961):110-7.

5 SHIDELER, Mary McDermott. "Bibliography." See 112.8, pp. 223-34.

CRITICAL AND BIOGRAPHICAL BOOKS

6 HADFIELD, Alice Mary. *An Introduction to Charles Williams.* London: Hale, 1959. [Biographical emphasis.]

7 HEATH-STUBBS, John. *Charles Williams.* London: Longmans, Green, 1955. [British Council pamphlet.] *

8 SHIDELER, Mary McDermott. *The Theology of Romantic Love: A Study in the Writings of Charles Williams.* New York: Harper, 1962.*

9 SHIDELER, Mary McDermott. *Charles Williams: A Critical Essay.* Grand Rapids, Mich.: Eerdmans, 1966. [Includes selected bibliography.]

CRITICAL ESSAYS

10 AUDEN, W. H. "Charles Williams: A Review Article." *Christian Century* 73(May 2, 1956):552-4.*

11 BORROW, Antony. "The Affirmation of Images, an Examination of the Novels of Charles Williams." *Nine*, 3,iv(1952):325-54.*

12 CONQUEST, Robert. "The Art of the Enemy." *EIC* 7(1957):42-55. [For debate on this article see "The Art of the Enemy." *EIC* 7(1957):330-43.]

13 CROWLEY, Cornelius P. "The Structural Pattern of Charles Williams' *Descent into Hell.*" *PMASAL* 39(1953):421-8.

14 HARTLEY, L. P. "The Novels of Charles Williams." *Time and Tide* 27(June 14, 1947):628-30.

15 HEPPENSTALL, Rayner. "The Works of Charles Williams." *New Statesman and Nation 37(May 21, 1949):532, 534.*

16 IRWIN, W. R. "There and Back Again: The Romances of Williams, Lewis and Tolkien." *SR* 69(1961):566-78.*

17 LA LANDE, Sister M., S.S.N.D. "Williams' Pattern of Time in *Descent into Hell.*" *Ren* 15(1963):88-95.

1 LEWIS, C. S. "Preface." *Essays Presented to Charles Williams.* Ed. Geoffrey Cumberlege. London: Oxford U P, 1947, pp. v-xiv.

2 MOORMAN, Charles. *Arthurian Triptych.* Berkeley: U of California P, 1960, pp. 38-101.

3 MOORMAN, Charles. *The Precincts of Felicity: Thy Augustinian City of the Oxford Christians.* Gainesville, Fla.: U of Florida P, 1966, pp. 19-29, 30-64, and *passim.**

4 PITT, Valerie. "Charles Williams: The Affirmation of Images." *Mandrake* 3(May 1946):27-33.

5 RIDLER, Anne. "Critical Introduction." See 112.2, pp. ix-lxxii.*

6 SALE, Roger. "England's Parnassus: C. S. Lewis, Charles Williams, and J. R. R. Tolkien." *HudR* 17(1964):203-25.*

7 WAIN, John. *Sprightly Running: Part of an Autobiography.* New York: St. Martin's, pp. 147-53. [Reminiscences of Williams at Oxford.]

8 WANDALL, Frederick S. "Charles Williams." See 81.10, Hoyt, pp. 121-34.

9 WINSHIP, G. P., Jr. "This Rough Magic: The Novels of Charles Williams." *YR* 40(1950):285-96.*

Angus Wilson (1913-)

TEXTS

10 *Anglo-Saxon Attitudes.* Foreword by F. Kermode. New York: Signet NAL, 1969.†

11 *The Wild Garden: Or Speaking of Writing.* London: Secker and Warburg, 1963. Berkeley and Los Angeles: U of California P, 1969.†

12 *Emile Zola: An Introductory Study of His Novels.* London: Secker and Warburg, 1952. 2d rev. ed., 1964. [Contains comments pertinent to Wilson's own writing.]

13 "Evil in the English Novel." 1, "Richardson and Jane Austen." 2, "George Eliot to Virginia Woolf." 3, "Outside the Central Tradition." 4, "Evil and the Novelist Today." *Listener* 68(1962):1079-80; 69(1963):15-6; 69(1963):63-5; 69(1963):115-7. [Shorter versions of Wilson's Northcliffe Lectures on this topic.]

BIBLIOGRAPHIES

For selected bibliography see below, Halio, 113.14, and Rabinovitz, 114.10.

CRITICAL AND BIOGRAPHICAL BOOKS

14 HALIO, Jay L. *Angus Wilson.* Edinburgh and London: Oliver and Boyd, 1964.

CRITICAL ESSAYS

1 BRADBURY, Malcolm. "The Short Stories of Angus Wilson." *SSF* 3(1966): 117-25.

2 COCKSHUT, A.O.J. "Favored Sons: The Moral World of Angus Wilson." *EIC* 9(1959):50-60.

3 COX, C. B. "Angus Wilson: Studies in Depression." See 13.11, pp. 117-53.

4 DRESCHER, Horst W. "Angus Wilson: An Interview." *NS* 17(1968):351-6. [Comments on *Late Call.*]

5 EDELSTEIN, Arthur. "Angus Wilson: The Territory Behind." See 16.16, Shapiro, pp. 144-61.

6 GINDIN, James. "The Reassertion of the Personal." *TQ*, 1,iv(1958):126-34.

7 KERMODE, Frank. "Mr. Wilson's People." See 16.6, pp. 193-7.*

8 MILLGATE, Michael. "Angus Wilson." *Writers at Work: The Paris Review Interviews.* Ed. Malcolm Cowley. New York: Viking, 1964, pp. 251-66.

9 POSTON, Lawrence. "A Conversation with Angus Wilson." *BA* 40(1966): 29-31.

10 RABINOVITZ, R. "Angus Wilson." See 8.21, pp. 64-96. [See also bibliography, pp. 185-95.]

11 RAYMOND, John. "Meg Eliot Surprised." *The Doge of Dover and Other Essays.* London: Macgibbon and Kee, 1960, pp. 170-8.

12 SCOTT-KILVERT, Ian. "Angus Wilson." *REL* 1,ii(1960):42-53.

13 VALLETTE, J. "Angus Wilson un peu par lui-même." *MdF* 334,no. 1142(1958):313-6.

Virginia Woolf (1882-1941)

TEXTS

14 Uniform Edition. London: Hogarth, 1929- . [Includes all of the novels, *A Haunted House and Other Stories*, and some volumes of essays. There are numerous reprints both English and American of individual works by Virginia Woolf, for example *Jacob's Room, Mrs. Dalloway, To the Lighthouse, Orlando, The Waves.*]

15 *Collected Essays.* Ed. Leonard Woolf. 4 vols. London: Hogarth, 1966-1967. [Includes all of the essays in six previously published volumes.]

16 *A Writer's Diary: Being Extracts from the Diary of Virginia Woolf.* Ed. Leonard Woolf. London: Hogarth, 1953. [These extracts from Virginia Woolf's diary written between 1915 and 1941 are limited chiefly to comments on her writing.] †

1 *Contemporary Writers.* Preface by Jean Guiguet. London: Hogarth, 1965. [Woolf essays and reviews on contemporary fiction.]

2 *Virginia Woolf and Lytton Strachey: Letters.* Ed. Leonard Woolf and James Strachey. London: Hogarth and Chatto and Windus; New York: Harcourt, Brace, 1956.

3 *Diary, January-May, 1905.* Berg Collection, New York. [The Berg Collection, New York Public Library, holds Virginia Woolf notebooks and typescripts for some novels and other works.]

BIBLIOGRAPHIES

4 BEEBE, Maurice. "Criticism of Virginia Woolf: A Selected Checklist with an Index to Studies of Separate Works." *MFS*, 2,i(1956):36-45.*

5 KIRKPATRICK, B. J. *Bibliography of Virginia Woolf.* London: Hart-Davis, 1957; rev. ed., 1967.*

CRITICAL AND BIOGRAPHICAL BOOKS

6 BADENHAUSEN, Ingeborg. *Die Sprache Virginia Woolfs: Ein Beitrag zur Stilistik des modernen englischen Romans.* Marburg (Lahn): Ebel, n.d.

7 BENNETT, Joan. *Virginia Woolf: Her Art as a Novelist.* Cambridge: Cambridge U P, 1945.*†

8 BLACKSTONE, Bernard. *Virginia Woolf: A Commentary.* London: Hogarth, 1949.

9 CHAMBERS, R. L. *The Novels of Virginia Woolf.* Edinburgh: Oliver and Boyd, 1947.*

10 CHASTAING, Maxime. *La philosophie de Virginia Woolf.* Paris: Presses Universitaires de France, 1951.

11 DAICHES, David. *Virginia Woolf.* Norfolk, Conn.: New Directions, 1942.*†

12 DELATTRE, Floris. *Le roman psychologique de Virginia Woolf.* Paris: Vrin, 1932.

13 FORSTER, E. M. *Virginia Woolf.* Cambridge: Cambridge U P, 1942.

14 GUIGUET, Jean. *Virginia Woolf and Her Works.* London: Hogarth, 1965.*

15 HAFLEY, James. *The Glass Roof: Virginia Woolf as Novelist.* New York: Russell and Russell, 1963.*

16 LEASKA, Mitchell A. *Virginia Woolf's Lighthouse: A Study in Critical Method.* London: Hogarth, 1970.

17 PIPPETT, Aileen. *The Moth and the Star: A Biography of Virginia Woolf.* Boston: Little, Brown, 1955. [Not definitive but contains letters.]

18 THAKUR, N. C. *The Symbolism of Virginia Woolf.* London: Oxford U P, 1965.

1 WOODRING, Carl. *Virginia Woolf.* New York: Columbia U P, 1966. [Columbia Essays on Modern Writers.] *

2 WOOLF, Leonard. *Sowing: An Autobiography of the Years 1880-1904. Growing: An Autobiography of the Years 1904-1911. Beginning Again: An Autobiography of the Years 1911-1918. Downhill All the Way: An Autobiography of the Years 1919-1939. The Journey Not the Arrival Matters.* London: Hogarth, 1960, 1961, 1964, 1967, 1969. [Valuable biographical commentary.] *

CRITICAL ESSAYS
The first title is a collection.

3 *MFS* 2,i(February 1956). Virginia Woolf special number.

4 ANNAN, Noel. *Leslie Stephen: His Thought and Character in Relation to His Time.* Cambridge, Mass.: Harvard U P, 1952, *passim.* [Numerous references to Virginia Woolf.] *

5 ARANJO, Victor de. " 'A Haunted House'–The Shattered Glass." *SSF* 3(1966):157-64.

6 AUERBACH, Erich. "The Brown Stocking." See 9.7, pp. 463-88.*

7 BECK, Warren. "For Virginia Woolf." See 10.9, O'Connor, pp. 243-54.*

8 BEJA, Morris. "Matches Struck in the Dark: Virginia Woolf's Moments of Vision." *CritQ* 6(1964):137-52.

9 BENJAMIN, Anna S. "Towards an Understanding of the Meaning of Virginia Woolf's *Mrs. Dalloway.*" *WSCL* 6(1965):214-27.

10 BEVIS, Dorothy. "*The Waves:* A Fusion of Symbol, Style and Thought in Virginia Woolf." *TCL* 2(1956):5-20.

11 BLOTNER, Joseph. "Mythic Patterns in *To the Lighthouse.*" *PMLA* 71(1956):547-62.*

12 BORD, Elizabeth F. "Luriana, Lurilee." *N&Q* 208(1963):380-1.

13 BOWEN, Elizabeth. See 19.9, pp. 71-82.

14 BRADBROOK, M. C. "Notes on the Style of Virginia Woolf." *Scrutiny* 1,i(1932):33-8.*

15 BROWER, Reuben A. "Something Central Which Permeated: Virginia Woolf and *Mrs. Dalloway.*" See 42.7, pp. 123-37.

16 CECIL, Lord David. "Virginia Woolf." See 42.10, pp. 160-80.

17 CHURCH, Margaret. "The Moment and Virginia Woolf." See 11.6, pp. 67-101.

18 CORNWELL, Ethel F. "Virginia Woolf's Moment of Reality." See 13.9, pp. 159-207.

19 EMPSON, William. "Virginia Woolf." *Scrutinies.* Ed. Edgell Rickword. London: Wishart, 1931, II, pp. 203-16.

20 FORTIN, René E. "Sacramental Imagery in *Mrs. Dalloway.*" *Ren* 18,i(1965):23-31.

1 FREEDMAN, Ralph. "Awareness and Fact: The Lyrical Vision in Virginia Woolf." See 13.14, pp. 185-270.*

2 FRIEDMAN, Norman. "The Waters of Annihilation: Double Vision in *To the Lighthouse.*" *ELH* 22(March 1955):61-79.*

3 GARNETT, David. "Virginia Woolf." *ASch* 34(1965):371-86.

4 GOLDMAN, Mark. "Virginia Woolf and the Critic as Reader." *PMLA* 80(1965):275-84.*

5 GRAHAM, John. "The 'Caricature Value' of Parody and Phantasy in *Orlando.*" *UTQ* 30(1961):345-66.*

6 GRAHAM, John. "A Negative Note on Bergson and Virginia Woolf." *EIC* 6(1956):70-4.

7 GRAHAM, John. "Point of View in *The Waves:* Some Services of the Style." *UTQ* 39,iii(1970):193-211.

8 GRAHAM, John. "Time in the Novels of Virginia Woolf." *UTQ* 18(1949): 186-201.*

9 GRAHAM, John. "Virginia Woolf and E. M. Forster: A Critical Dialogue." *TSLL* 7(1966):387-400.*

10 HAVARD-WILLIAMS, Peter and Margaret. "*Bateau Ivre*: The Symbol of the Sea in Virginia Woolf's *The Waves.*" *ES* 34(1953):9-17.

11 HAVARD-WILLIAMS, Peter and Margaret. "Mystical Experience in Virginia Woolf's *The Waves.*" *EIC* 4,i(1954):71-84.

12 HILDICK, Wallace. "In That Solitary Room." *KR* 27(1965):302-17.*

13 HOFFMANN, Charles. "The 'Real' Mrs. Dalloway." *UKCR* 22,iii(1956): 204-8.

14 HUNGERFORD, Edward A. " 'My Tunnelling Process': The Method of *Mrs. Dalloway.*" *MFS* 3(1957):164-7.

15 JOHNSTONE, J. K. See 5.6, pp. 126-56, 320-73.

16 KING, Merton P. "*The Waves* and the Androgynous Mind." *University Review* 30(1963):128-34.

17 LEHMANN, John. "Virginia Woolf." See 29.19, pp. 23-33.

18 MELCHIORI, Giorgio. "The Moment as a Time Unit in Fiction." See 14.17, pp. 175-87.*

19 MOODY, A. D. "The Unmasking of Clarissa Dalloway." *REL* 3(1962): 67-79.

20 OCAMPO, Victoria. "Virginia Woolf, Orlando y Cia." *Sur* (Buenos Aires), 1938. [Chiefly reminiscence.]

21 OVERCARSH, F. L. "The Lighthouse, Face to Face." *Accent* 10(Winter 1950):107-23.

22 PEDERSEN, Glenn. "Vision in *To the Lighthouse.*" *PMLA* 73(1958): 585-600.

23 RANTAVAARA, Irma. "On Romantic Imagery in Virginia Woolf's *The Waves* with Special Reference to Antithesis." *NM* 60(1959):72-89.

1 ROBERTS, John H. "Vision and Design in Virginia Woolf." *PMLA* 61(1946):835-47.*

2 SIMON, Irène. "Some Aspects of Virginia Woolf's Imagery." *ES* 41(1960): 180-96.

3 STANZEL, Franz. "Die Erzählsituationen in Virginia Woolf's *Jacob's Room, Mrs. Dalloway* and *To the Lighthouse.*" *GRM* 35(1954):196-213.*

4 TOYNBEE, Philip. "Virginia Woolf: A Study of Three Experimental Novels." *Horizon* 14(November 1946):290-304.*

5 TROY, William. "Virginia Woolf and the Novel of Sensibility." See 77.13, Hyman, pp. 65-88.*

6 WILKINSON, Ann. "A Principle of Unity in *Between the Acts.*" *Criticism* 8(1966):53-63.*

7 WRIGHT, Nathalia. "*Mrs. Dalloway:* A Study in Composition." *CE* 5(1944): 351-8.

NOTES

INDEX

INDEX

INDEX

INDEX H–K

INDEX

INDEX

INDEX

INDEX

GOLDENTREE BIBLIOGRAPHIES
IN LANGUAGE AND LITERATURE

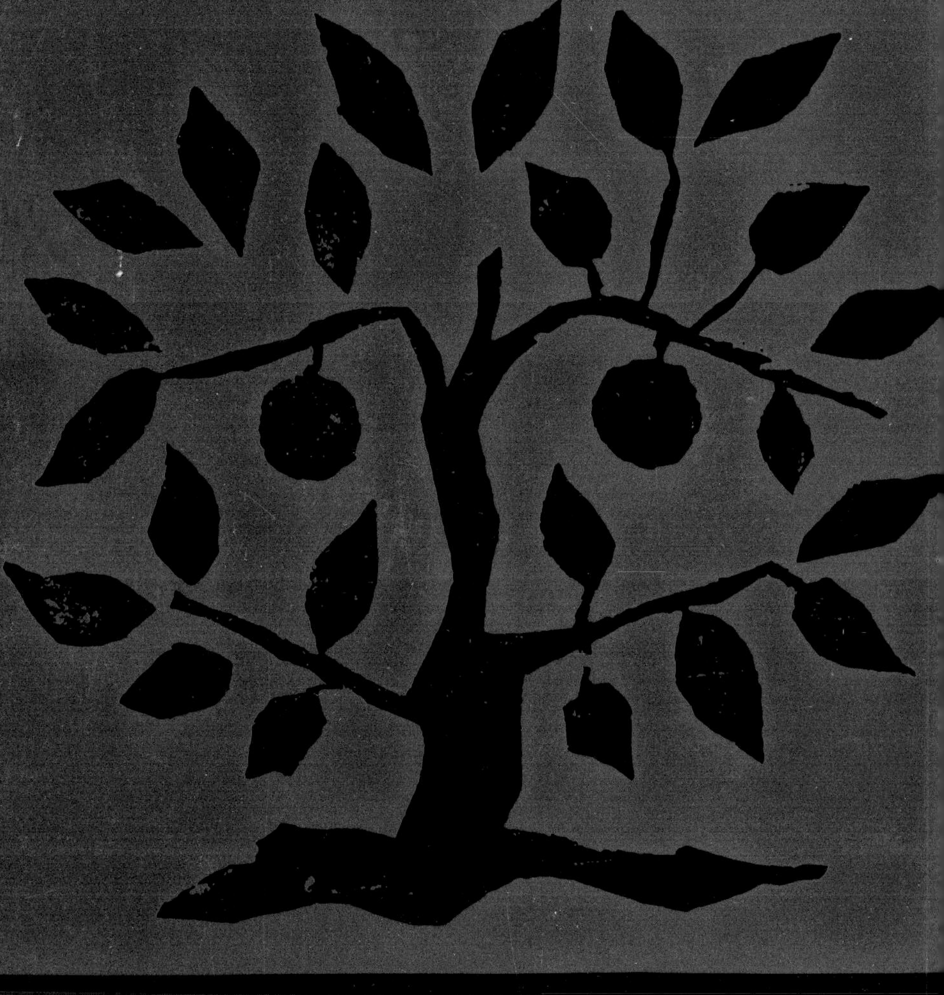

AHM PUBLISHING CORPORATION